Ganbatte Means Go For It!

or...How to Become an English Teacher in Japan

By Celeste Heiter

**THINGS
ASIAN
PRESS**

Published by ThingsAsian Press   www.thingsasian.com

This book is dedicated to the adventurer and the teacher in all of us.

Contents

Foreword 1
Acknowledgments 3
Introduction 5
Do You Have What It Takes? 21
The Contemporary Job Market 31
Making the Move 37
Researching from Home 57
Arriving in Japan 69
Landing a Job in Japan 77
Finding a Place to Live 85
Getting a Work Visa 95
Teaching English 103
Survival Tips 111
Cultural Do's & Don'ts 121
Resources, Bibliography, Webliography, & Glossary 127
Afterword: Vignettes of Japan 145

Seven Japanese Proverbs

Vision without action is a daydream. Action without vision is a nightmare.

If you understand everything, you must be misinformed.

The reverse side also has a reverse side.

When you have completed 95% of your journey you are halfway there.

Fall down seven times, stand up eight.

If you look up, there are no limits.

To teach is to learn.

Map of Japan

HOKKAIDO

• Sapporo

HONSHU

• Sendai

Kanazawa•

TOKYO
Yokohama• Kawasaki
Kamakura

Nagoya•

Kobe• Kyoto
Osaka

Hiroshima•

Matsuyama• Takamatsu

SHIKOKU

Fukuoka• Kitakyushu

Nagasaki•

KYUSHU

Foreword

Many years ago, when I was a child of four or five years old, I saw a picture of the *Dai Butsu*, the great statue of Buddha that has stood in the town of Kamakura, Japan for more than 750 years. The picture I saw was an illustration in volume three of a set of *Golden Book Encyclopedias* under the heading for Buddha. And although I came from a Catholic family and knew nothing of Buddhism until much later in life, that picture beckoned to me. I had the feeling that someday I would go to Kamakura to see that great statue...And one day, I did.

My journey to Japan began in the town of St. Helena, California, in the heart of the Napa Valley, where I was the proprietor of a small tailoring business. One spring afternoon, Mark Raus, a man I'd met at an Oktoberfest celebration a few months earlier, came into my shop with some clothing in need of repairs. I was newly single and so was he, so when he asked me go with him to the symphony in San Francisco, I said yes. On our date, he told me of his travels in Europe, and of his desire to embark on another adventure, this time to Japan. He had a friend who was there teaching English in Tokyo.

Over the next few months, our relationship blossomed, and the next thing we knew, we were 35,000 feet over the Pacific Ocean, on a 747 bound for Narita Airport. Little did I know just how profoundly that journey would shape the rest of my life.

Upon our arrival in Tokyo, Mark's English-teaching friend Bruce Whistler extended us his generous hospitality. Within two weeks of our arrival, we were both employed as full-time English conversation instructors at Gakken White House, and shortly thereafter, we found a furnished apartment that we could afford on our salaries. In the two years that followed, we spent our afternoons and evenings teaching English in a conversation salon, and our weekends and vacations seeing as much of the country as our time and budget would allow. And of course, our very first outing was a visit to the *Dai Butsu* at Kamakura.

An unexpected detour in our plans occurred when I discovered that I was pregnant. But instead of hightailing it back to the States, we decided to stay and have the baby in Japan. This turned out to be a wise and wonderful choice. There was a rainbow over Tokyo the day our beautiful baby boy was born. We named him Will.

Mark went on to become faculty supervisor at Gakken White House; and a few months after Will was born, I returned with him to visit my mother in my hometown of Mobile, Alabama. When Mark completed his contract with Gakken, we were reunited in Mobile, and returned shortly thereafter to the Napa Valley.

Japan Airlines has a flight-training center at Napa's tiny airport. Each year, dozens of Japan Airlines flight instructors, counselors and administrators come to Napa with their families, where they live, work and attend school. Since our return from Japan, Mark and I have both worked as private English tutors to these Japanese families. And although we have now gone our separate ways, we remain friends and dedicated parents to our son Will. Our lives have been irrevocably etched and will always be defined by the experiences that we shared in that remarkable culture.

If you are reading this book, chances are you have your own dream of going to Japan. Whatever your reason, these pages contain a trove of information that you can use to turn that dream into your life story.

Seiko o inorimasu,

Celeste Heiter

Acknowledgements

I would like to express my appreciation to the following individuals for their generous contributions toward the creation of Ganbatte:

To my friend and publisher, Albert Wen, for giving me the opportunity to write this book, and for underwriting its publication.

To my son Will, for being my life's greatest treasure, and the best thing that happened to me while I was in Japan.

To René Pulido, for his love, support and patience throughout this project, and always.

To Mark Raus, for inspiring me to go to Japan in the first place, and for sharing the experience with me.

To the Shimizu Family (Masaki, Yuko, Hiroki, Takae, Hideki, Toshie, and Mariko), for being our home away from home in Japan.

To Mrs. Hiroko Ito, her husband Katsuhiko Ito, and their sons Ryosuke and Kosuke, for generously supplying me with important research materials and information, and for being one of the loveliest families in all of Japan.

To Barry Gjerde, Frank Lev, and Ralph Hardimon, for providing me with reliable, first-hand, up-to-the-minute information on the details of daily life in Japan.

To Luis Poza, for his excellent website, and for being a good friend and fellow teacher in Tokyo.

To all my former students, the staff at Gakken White House, and the people of Japan, for making my stay in your wonderful country a truly memorable one that has enriched my life in immeasurable ways.

Reader's Notes

The Japanese language uses no plurals. For example, *tatami*, the Japanese word for a woven rice-straw mat, is the same whether it is used to denote a single floor panel, or a whole room full of them. Never "*tatamis*." Therefore, even when used to convey plural objects, Japanese words used within this text will appear in singular form only.

Most of the Japanese words that appear in this text will be used in such a way as to convey their meaning contextually. Therefore, except when deemed necessary, there will be no in-line translations for Japanese words. For easy reference, a glossary of Japanese terminology is included in Chapter Twelve.

All Internet links included in the text are valid as of the time this book goes to press. However, please note that the World Wide Web is perpetually evolving, and therefore, some links may have changed or expired.

All currency conversions used within this text are based on a long-term average. The actual dollar/yen value varies from week to week, day to day, and even from minute to minute. Therefore, the currency values cited in this text are for the purpose of making general estimates only.

Introduction

So you want to teach English in Japan?

Well…take it from one who's done just that – pack your bags, pull up your socks, and get ready for the experience of a lifetime.

Japan is a culture unlike any other. For starters, they squeeze a population half that of the United States into a stunningly beautiful land mass not much larger than the state of California, and somehow manage to coexist peacefully. The Japanese people can be, at once, ultra-conservative yet daringly avant-garde. And remarkably, they seamlessly integrate their ancient and deeply ingrained traditions into an otherwise futuristic lifestyle. A year teaching English in Japan will forever change the way you look at life and the world at large.

The Die is Cast

Let's assume, for starters, that you don't need convincing. You've thought it over; you've browsed vicariously through an armload of opulent travel brochures, resplendent with Buddhist temples, lofty mountain peaks and tatami tea rooms, and have decided that *Eigo no sensei* is the job for you. Believe it or not, in the smorgasbord that is the 21st-century job market, singling out a career choice from such a bewildering array of options is a major step forward.

I wish I could tell you that the rest is easy, but there's a vast expanse between saying you'd like to teach English in Japan, and actually greeting your first student in that English conversation salon way over there on the other side of the Pacific Ocean. The process requires an enormous amount of research, planning, organizing, patience, finances, and hard work. Nevertheless, with a goodly measure of faith, courage and perseverance, becoming an English teacher in Japan is an attainable goal.

The Four Elements

The process of becoming an English Teacher in Japan can be divided into four elements or phases (roughly, but not necessarily, in this order):

- Prepping, Packing and Psyching,

- Getting Settled in a Brave New World

- Finding a Way to Earn Your Daily *Gohan*

- Immigration *Nihon-do*.

Each of these four elements will play a crucial role in the success and enjoyment of your Japan experience, from how well equipped you are with life's essentials to your eventual success in getting hired and finding a place to live.

Prepping, Packing and Psyching

This is the initial phase of your journey. It includes tasks such as studying the language and culture, getting your passport and paperwork in order, researching the job market, making arrangements for your domestic affairs while you're away, deciding what to take with you, making your travel arrangements, and preparing yourself physically and psychologically for the experience. The more mindfully and thoroughly you prepare, the more comfortable, and organized you will be once you've arrived in Japan. Chapter Two contains a list of pre-travel tips and suggestions, as well as a timeline to help you complete all your preparations in time for your departure date.

Getting Settled in a Brave New World

Traveling to Japan is a unique experience, and the process of making a permanent move and integrating yourself into the culture can be especially trying. Moreover, the process of moving to Japan is twofold: First, finding a place to lay your head for the first few days or weeks; and ultimately, landing a place that you can afford and would be willing to call home for awhile. And unless your employment and living accommodations have already been arranged before you travel, a good initial home base from which to commence your job and apartment search is the single best asset you could wish for. Accommodations and customs in Japan are vastly different from those in the United States and Europe, and each step in the process presents its own unique challenges. Chapters Four and Six address the gambit of finding lodgings and a permanent address in more detail.

Finding a Way to Earn Your Daily Gohan

The decade of the 1980's and early 1990's is sometimes referred to as the "Bubble Years" for English teachers in Japan. For those who were lucky enough to have been a part of that golden era, the classifieds were filled with page after page of job opportunities, and a qualified candidate could pick and choose from among dozens of teaching positions. However, due to a downturn in the Japanese economy in recent years, the current job market may appear somewhat less abundant than it used to be. And although this can present a challenging hurdle, it is no cause for trepidation. Japan has an ever-burgeoning economy, with ample opportunities for the dedicated job seeker. Chapter Five has the latest information for conducting a successful job search in today's economy.

Immigration Nihon-do

For a time in Japan, during the aforementioned "Bubble Years," a tourist visa could be converted to a work visa right on the spot at the Immigration Office in downtown Tokyo. Unfortunately, the Japanese government has since decided to revert to its former system, which requires that foreigners apply for their work visas at a consulate or embassy outside Japan. While these strictures can be costly and exacting, in the interest of landing a lucrative teaching position and embarking upon a once-in-a-lifetime adventure, it's well worth the effort. Also, keep in mind that it is possible to purchase a segmented airline ticket that will allow you to include your visa run in your itinerary. Remember too that many teaching positions include a work visa as part of the benefits package, in which case your employer will guide you through he process. But if the company that hires you does not provide you with a work visa, Chapter Seven contains a step-by-step description of the process required to secure one.

An Overview of Japan

The nation of Japan is made up of many islands, however, only five of them are largely inhabited: Honshu, the largest and most populous; Shikoku, a much smaller island nestled into Honshu's southeastern shore; Kyushu, a slightly larger island located at Honshu's southern tip; Hokkaido, a large island to the north; and Okinawa, a tiny, isolated island far to the south.

Honshu

As Japan's main landmass, Honshu includes the cities of Tokyo, Yokohama, Nagoya, Kyoto, Kobe, Osaka, Hiroshima, Nikko, and Sendai, as well as hundreds of smaller cities, towns and villages. Much of the central landscape is steeply mountainous and unsuitable for habitation or farming, therefore the majority of Japan's population is concentrated in cities located on the coastal Kansai and Kanto plains.

Tokyo

The largest of Japan's metropolitan areas, Tokyo actually encompasses dozens of large satellite cities and suburbs. This bustling metropolis is the center of trade, industry, government and education.

POPULATION: Approximately 8 million
INDUSTRIES: All types
ATTRACTIONS: The Imperial Palace, Meiji Shrine, Asakusa Kannon Temple, Tokyo Tower, Tokyo Disneyland, Tokyo Dome, Ueno Zoo, Yoyogi Park, Roppongi Nightlife, Ginza Shopping, Metropolitan Art Museum, National Museum of Modern Art, Kabukiza Theater, Sumo at Ryogoku Kokugikan, Sunshine 60 Tower, Shinagawa Prince Hotel Ice Rink (to name only a few of the thousands of sites to enjoy in Tokyo).
NEAREST AIRPORT: Tokyo Narita International Airport (NRT)
WEBSITE: **www.tcvb.or.jp/**

Yokohama

Located on the western shores of Tokyo Bay, Yokohama is one of Tokyo's most important satellite cities. In addition to being Japan's largest seaport, Yokohama is a highly cosmopolitan environment on the leading edge of technology and international business.

POPULATION: Approximately 3.5 million
INDUSTRIES: Technology, research, manufacturing, shipping, chemicals, food products.
ATTRACTIONS: Yamashita Park and Port, Yokohama Chinatown, Yokohama Stadium,
Yokohama Foreign Cemetery, CosmoWorld Amusement Park,
Yokohama Museum of Art, the Silk Center, Sankei Garden.
NEAREST AIRPORT: Tokyo Narita International Airport (NRT)
WEBSITE: **www.city.yokohama.jp/**

Osaka

The city of Osaka, Japan's third largest metropolis, is located on the south central coast of Honshu. Industry and commerce, much of which is wholesale, are the mainstays of the local economy. The city is a patchwork of traditional and modern architecture and features a network of canals.

POPULATION: Approximately 2.5 million
INDUSTRIES: Pharmaceuticals, textiles, notions, toys, confectionery,
chemicals, machinery, fashion, and biotechnology.
ATTRACTIONS: Osaka Castle, National Bunraku Theater, Tsutenkaku Tower,
Tennoji Zoo, Kaiyukan Aquarium, Tempozan Resort, Cosmo Square, Osaka Dome,
Dotombori Entertainment District, Shinsaibashi Shopping District.
NEAREST AIRPORT: Kansai International Airport (KIAC)
WEBSITE: **www.city.osaka.jp/**

Kanazawa

Situated on the Sai and Asano Rivers, and surrounded by the Japan Alps, Kanazawa is a western coastal city of great natural beauty, known for the exceptional quality of its traditional commodities and unique crafts.

Population: Approximately 450,000
Industries: Pottery, lacquerware, gold leaf, silk, rice, sake,
and traditional foods, tourism and light industry.
Attractions: Myoryuji Temple, Kenrokuen Garden, Nagamachi
Samurai District, Eastern Temple Quarter, Eastern Pleasure Quarter.
Nearest Airport: Komatsu Airport (domestic only)
Website: **www.city.kanazawa.ishikawa.jp/kanazawaE.html**

Nagoya

Nagoya, the fourth largest city in Japan, is located on Ise Bay, at the heart of central Japan, amid a rich natural landscape, including the Nobi Plain, and the Kiso River. Nagoya is one of Japan's major cities, and an important industrial and cultural center.

Population: Approximately 2 million
Industries: Manufacturing, Export, Fashion, Agriculture, Fishing
Attractions: Nagoya Castle, Inuyama Castle, Atsuta Shrine,
Shirotori Gardern, Port of Nagoya Aquarium, Tokugawa Art Museum,
Higashiyama Sky Tower, Cormorant Fishing on the Kiso River
Nearest Airport: Nagoya International Airport
Website: **www.city.nagoya.jp/**

Kobe

Best known for its world famous beef and Japan's finest sake, Kobe is a significant gateway to the world. Home of the International Business Support Center for foreign companies conducting business in Kobe, and the Kobe Medical Industry Development Project, it is also a burgeoning commercial metropolis.

POPULATION: Approximately 1.5 million
INDUSTRIES: Steel production, shipping and shipbuilding, chemicals, rubber, trading houses, pearls, apparel, shoes, furniture, food products, agriculture and aquaculture.
ATTRACTIONS: Kobe Port Tower and Museum, Kobe Chinatown, Ikuta Entertainment District, Kobe City Museum, Kitano Trade District, Mt. Rokko and the Inland Sea National Park.
NEAREST AIRPORT: Kansai International Airport (KICA)
WEBSITE: **www.city.kobe.jp/**

Kyoto

Formerly the ancient capital of Japan, Kyoto is a highly cultural and opulently beautiful inland city built on the slopes of Mt. Hiei. Kyoto and the satellite towns of Nara and Ohara are the home of countless shrines, temples, gardens and national treasures.

POPULATION: Approximately 1.5 million
INDUSTRIES: Tourism, traditional crafts and food products, manufacturing, publishing.
ATTRACTIONS: Kyoto Imperial Park and Palace, Nijo Castle, Daitokuji Temple,
Kinkakuji and Ginkakuji (the Golden and Silver Pavillions), Ryoanji Rock and Sand Garden,
Heian Shrine, Kyomizu Temple, Kyoto Botanical Gardens, Kyoto Zoo (This is by no means the complete list of things to see in Kyoto.)
NEAREST AIRPORT: Kansai International Airport (KICA)
WEBSITE: **www.city.kyoto.jp/**

Kawasaki

Another of Tokyo's satellite cities, Kawasaki is located on Tokyo Bay between Tokyo and Yokohama. It is a major shipping port and home of the high-tech Kawasaki Microcomputer City.

POPULATION: Approximately 1.25 million
INDUSTRIES: Shipping, manufacturing, technology
ATTRACTIONS: Heigen Temple, Hirama Temple, Ozen Temple,
Mukogaoka Playground, Daishi Park, Yumemigasaki Zoo, Todoroki Arena,
Kawasaki Civic Museum, Citizens Plaza, Japanese House Museum.
NEAREST AIRPORT: Tokyo Narita International Airport (NRT)
WEBSITE: **www.city.kawasaki.jp/**

Hiroshima

Marked for perpetuity as the site of the first atomic bomb in human history, Hiroshima is a thriving city that embodies a relentless quest for world peace. With the Peace Memorial as its focus, the city of Hiroshima is a modern metropolis with a flourishing economy.

POPULATION: Approximately 1.25 million
INDUSTRIES: Tourism, manufacturing, technology, international trade.
ATTRACTIONS: Hiroshima Peace Memorial, Memorial Cathedral for World Peace,
Hiroshima Castle, Shukkei Garden, Asa Zoo, Hiroshima Botanical Gardens, Miyajima Island
NEAREST AIRPORT: Hiroshima International Airport (HIJ)
WEBSITE: **www.city.hiroshima.jp/**

Sendai

Now the largest city and commercial center in the Tohoku Region, Sendai is the regional seat of federal administrative agencies. Sendai is also a rail hub near the shipping port of Shiogama in the southwestern corner of Matsushima Bay.

POPULATION: Approximately 1 million
INDUSTRIES: Industrial manufacturing, shipping, technology,
food processing, fishing, agriculture, local crafts.
ATTRACTIONS: Sendai International Center, Sendai Science Museum,
Sendai Astronomical Observatory, Sendai City Museum, Ancient Tomizawa Ruins.
NEAREST AIRPORT: Tokyo Narita International Airport (NAR)
WEBSITE: **www.city.sendai.jp/**

Kyushu

The third largest of Japan's four main islands, Kyushu is little more than a mile off the coast of Honshu and is connected by bridge, tunnel and rail. It was once an important cultural gateway to the continent of Asia, and its landscape is defined by four active volcanic mountain ranges.

Kitakyushu

The port city of Kitakyushu is actually a unification of five older cities, each with its own unique characteristics. Located at the northern end of the island, just off the tip of Honshu, Kitakyushu is now an important industrial city.

POPULATION: Approximately 1 million
INDUSTRIES: Iron, steel, manufacturing, technology, chemicals, publishing, food processing, local crafts.
ATTRACTIONS: Mekari Shrine, Kokura Castle, Old Moji Port, Space World, Hiraodai Park
NEAREST AIRPORT: Fukuoka International Airport (FUK)
WEBSITE: **www.city.kitakyushu.jp/**

Fukuoka

The city of Fukuoka, also known as Hakata, is not only the center of administration and economy in Kyushu, but also a point of convergence for air routes and railroads. Now a state-of-the-art commercial city, Fukuoka is the site of many ancient ruins and historical treasures.

POPULATION: Approximately 1.25 million
INDUSTRIES: Manufacturing, textiles, food products, local crafts.
ATTRACTIONS: Hakozaki Hachiman Shrine, Sumiyoshi Shrine, Shofuku Temple, Kinryu Temple, Dazaifu Shrine, Kanzeon Temple, Higashi Park, Mongol Invasion Fortress Remains, Fukuoka Castle Remains, Fukuoka City Archeological Operation Center, local spas and hot springs.
NEAREST AIRPORT: Fukuoka International Airport (FUK)
WEBSITE: **www.city.fukuoka.jp/**

Nagasaki

Nagasaki and its surrounding area is made up of 971 inhabited and uninhabited islands. Nagasaki City, in the heart of Nagasaki-Hanto Peninsula, is a port city that extends up the slope of a steep mountain. Most notable as the site of the second atomic bomb in 1945, Nagasaki is once again a scenic and cosmopolitan city.

POPULATION: Approximately 450,000
INDUSTRIES: Manufacturing, steel, shipbuilding.
ATTRACTIONS: Peace Park, Ora Tenshudo Church, Madame Butterfly's Glover Mansion, Kujyuku-shima Island, Saikai National Park, Mt. Fugen-dake Volcano, Nagasaki Holland Village
NEAREST AIRPORT: Fukuoka International Airport (FUK)
WEBSITE: **www-cc.nagasaki-u.ac.jp/nagasaki-city/nagasaki.html**

Shikoku

Connected to the island of Honshu by the Seto Bridge, Shikoku is the smallest of Japan's four main islands. Mountainous and forested, the island is still largely rural with the exception of the cities of Takamatsu and Matsuyama. Shikoku is known for its Eighty-Eight Temple Pilgrimage.

Takamatsu

Originally a castle town in the feudal age, the city of Takamatsu has prospered as an important center of transportation for agricultural products.

POPULATION: Approximately 350,000
.INDUSTRIES: Cotton, sugar and salt (known as "Sanuki Sanpaku" - three whites)
ATTRACTIONS: Ritsurin Park, Sanuki Minegeikan Folk Art Museum, Zentsuji Temple, Entertainment District nightlife.
NEAREST AIRPORT: Kansai International Airport (KICA)
WEBSITE: **www.city.takamatsu.kagawa.jp/**

Matsuyama

While maintaining a country atmosphere, Matsuyama is an orderly, modern post-WWII reconstructed city, and Shikoku's largest. The city features cable cars as a means of local travel, and the surrounding countryside is one of great natural beauty.

POPULATION: Approximately 450,000
INDUSTRIES: Light manufacturing, agriculture, fishing, tourism, local crafts and foods
ATTRACTIONS: Matsuyama Castle, Dogo Onsen, Ishiteji Temple
NEAREST AIRPORT: Kansai International Airport (KICA)
WEBSITE: **www.city.matsuyama.ehime.jp/**

Hokkaido

Hokkaido is Japan's northernmost and second largest island. Connected to northern Honshu by the 33-mile Seikan Tunnel, Hokkaido is a sparsely populated, sub-arctic landscape of rugged and unspoiled beauty.

Sapporo
The city of Sapporo is the largest metropolitan area on the island of Hokkaido. Located on the west central coast, overlooking the Sea of Japan, much of Sapporo is mountainous with an urban concentration focused around the Toyohira River, which runs through the city.

POPULATION: Approximately 2 million
INDUSTRIES: Mining, manufacturing, construction, fishing, brewing, tourism
ATTRACTIONS: Odori Park, Migishi Kotaro Museum of Art, Hokkaido Museum of Modern Art, Hokkaido University Botanical Gardens, Pioneer Trail, Clock Tower, Historical Village of Hokkaido
NEAREST AIRPORT: Sapporo Chitose International Airport (CTS)
WEBSITE: **www.city.sapporo.jp/**

An Overview of Tokyo

The metropolis known as Tokyo is actually a conglomeration of several dozen cities whose boundaries have merged into each other over the past century. However, each of Tokyo's districts has its own distinct characteristics, cultural attributes, and commercial activities. To facilitate the daily business of inter-city commerce, the whole jigsaw puzzle is bound together by a circular commuter railway called the Yamanote. This remarkable transit system, operated by Japan Railway (JR), is 48.4 kilometers around and operates more than 600 trains that stop with near-precision punctuality at each of its 29 stations. At an average of two minutes between stops, the full circuit around the city of Tokyo takes just a little over an hour. To further enable busy commuters to travel freely about its many districts, the Yamanote is traversed by a network of smaller local railways and subways that provide access to both the heart and the periphery of the city.

'Round the Yamanote
Beginning with Tokyo Station, the 29 stops on the Yamanote Line are: Tokyo, Yurakucho, Shimbashi, Hamamatsucho, Tamachi, Shinagawa, Osaki, Gotanda, Meguro, Ebisu, Shibuya, Harajuku, Yoyogi, Shinjuku, Shin Okubo, Takadanobaba, Mejiro, Ikebukuro, Otsuka, Sugamo, Komagome, Tabata, Nishi Nippori, Nippori, Uguisudani, Ueno, Okamachi, Akihabara, and Kanda.

Tokyo's Major Districts
Central Tokyo – The very heart of Tokyo is the site of the Imperial Palace, which is the residence of Japan's reigning Emperor Akihito and his family. Although it is possible to walk around in the vicinity of the Imperial Palace, the public is only allowed inside the Imperial gates on two days of the year: January 2, and December 23, the Emperor's birthday.

Business District
Downtown Tokyo, the hub of business and government activities, is made up of several districts, including Akasaka, where the Parliament and other government buildings are located. Some other stations also located in the central business district of Tokyo are Kanda, Hibiya, Nihombashi, Yurakucho, and Tokyo Station itself.

Ginza
Probably best known for its opulent shopping and the finest of restaurants, the Ginza is another important area located in downtown Tokyo's business district.

Roppongi
When the sun sets on the city and the nightlife starts to sizzle, Roppongi is the place to see and be seen, at the hottest dance clubs and the latest in avant-garde performance arts.

Asakusa
Not to be confused with Akasaka, Asakusa is the site of one of Tokyo's oldest, largest and most important temples. Asakusa Kannon Temple is famous for the towering *torii* gate, with its huge red paper lantern marking the main entrance.

Shinjuku
One of Tokyo's busiest and most important commerical centers, Shinjuku's skyline of department stores, hotels and office buildings, rises high above the rest of the city. It includes the Mitsui Building, the Sumitomo Building, the Shinjuku Center Building, Keio Plaza, the Century Hyatt, the Tokyo Hilton, and the Shinjuku Prince. Department stores: Isetan, Mitsukoshi, Odakyo, and Keio, surround Shinjuku station, which is practically a small city in itself.

Ikebukuro
Home of Sunshine 60, a high-rise building that was once the tallest in Asia, Ikebukuro is a burgeoning suburban business district where several transit lines intersect. Here you will find some of Tokyo's largest department stores, including Tobu, Seibu, and Tokyu Hands, along with thousands of other businesses both large and small.

Harajuku
As the center of teen fashion, fad, and entertainment, Harajuku is a beehive of activity for Tokyo's youth. The streets around Harajuku station are lined with casual restaurants and trendy boutiques that sell pop-culture clothing, music, and lifestyle accessories.

Yoyogi
This popular Tokyo destination features Yoyogi Koen, a vast public park, where Japanese pop and rock bands, street performers, vendors and fashion mavens once used to strut their stuff, especially on Sunday afternoons. It's a little more tame these days, due to the protests of local residents. Yoyogi is also the home of the Yoyogi Sports Center, a remnant of the 1964 Olympics.

Ueno
Here you can visit Ueno Zoo and Ueno Park, which includes several of Japan's national art galleries and museums. Another not-to-miss feature of this district is the Ueno Fish Market, where commercial fishermen unload their catch each day, to be hawked and purveyed by the fishmongers in open market stalls. This lively enterprise makes for good free entertainment, and the seafood restaurants in the neighborhood are said to be the best in all of Tokyo. Ueno Park is also one of the best venues for viewing the cherry blossoms at *ohanami* time.

Akihabara
If you're in the market for anything electronic or electric, or just want to browse the latest in techno-gadgetry, Akihabara is the place to go. You'll be dazzled by its eye-popping shop windows and deafened by the cacophony of sirens, bells, whistles, beeps, and buzzers. It's also one of the few places in Tokyo where a bit of discreet haggling is acceptable.

Shibuya
In addition to being one of Tokyo's most popular shopping districts, Shibuya is the location of the Meiji Shrine, and also of one of Japan's most beloved landmarks, the statue of the faithful dog Hachiko. This Akita dog accompanied his master, Mr. Eisaburo Ueno, a college professor at the Imperial University, to Shibuya station each morning and awaited his return in the same spot each afternoon. When the professor was taken ill and died while at work one day in 1925, he never returned again to Shibuya Station. However, Hachiko continued to wait for him every afternoon for nearly ten years thereafter. Today, a statue of Hachiko stands in his honor, and is the landmark of choice for friends and lovers arranging a rendezvous in Tokyo. You can read a nicely written account of the tale of Hachiko at
www.metropolis.co.jp/biginjapanarchive349/303/biginjapaninc.htm

Shinagawa
Located at the southern nadir of the Yamanote Line, Shinagawa is a popular residential area and an important transit railway hub. There you will find the Kaian Temple, and a number of major hotels, including the Shinagawa Prince, which boasts Tokyo's most popular ice rink.

The Suburbs
Because of the prohibitively expensive cost of living in the city of Tokyo, outlying regions that are within a reasonable commute distance are popular residential areas. For the benefit of living in quieter, less crowded, and less costly surroundings, Tokyo commuters are willing to travel an hour or more by train to get to work or school. When asked where they live, many of your students may reply, Chiba, Saitama, Ibaraki, Kanagawa, or Gunma, the outlying prefectures that surround the city of Tokyo.

A Focus on Americans in Tokyo...But not Exclusively

Since this book is based largely on my first-hand experiences while living and teaching in Japan, its contents originate from the perspective of an American author. It is also focused on the Tokyo metropolitan area because, again, Tokyo is the city with which I am most familiar and offers an abundant and readily accessible job market. However, there are thousands of opportunities for native and fluent English speakers of any nationality, and these opportunities are available throughout all of Japan. The historic and picturesque city of Kyoto, as well as the cities of Nagoya, Osaka, Yokohama, Kanazawa, Sendai, Sapporo, Fukuoka, along with dozens of others, have a growing need for English teachers, and may provide a desirable alternative to the intensely urban experience one can expect from living in Tokyo.

But no matter where you come from or where you choose to seek your fortune, if you follow the steps and tips outlined in this book, with diligence, perseverance, faith, and a little luck, before you know it, you'll be earning your yen as an *Eigo no sensei* in Japan. Good Luck and Ganbatte!

Notes:

Do You Have What It Takes?

Making the choice to become an English teacher in Japan is not one to be taken lightly. The process requires an enormous expenditure of time, energy, effort and money; not to mention the fact that it comes with no guarantee. And although Japan is one of the most sophisticated, intriguing, and endearing nations in the world, the country, the culture, and the climate can present many difficulties for foreigners in the course of everyday life. Therefore, it is crucial that you take a thorough personal inventory to ensure that you have what it takes before embarking upon such a daring venture. The following questionnaire will help you assess your attributes and assets to determine if you are up to the challenge.

Questionnaire

1. My level of education is
a) Post Graduate Degree and/or TEFL Certificate
b) College Graduate
c) Some College
d) High School graduate

2. I have
a) More than $5000 in savings
b) $3500-5000 in savings
c) $1000-3500 in savings
d) Less than $1000 in savings

3. My physical condition is
a) Excellent in both stamina and overall physical health
b) A little out of shape but basically good
c) Fairly good but with a few troublesome health conditions
d) Lacking stamina and in need of regular medical attention

4. I am someone who
a) Can face any challenge without fear
b) Can get by on my own in most challenging situations
c) Functions best with a companion
d) Is easily frightened by unfamiliar settings or unexpected events

5. I am a person who
a) Enjoys new challenges and situations
b) Enjoys the unfamiliar, but prefers my routine
c) Avoids unfamiliar situations whenever possible
d) Must adhere to a strict and familiar routine

6. When faced with a challenge
a) I never give up until I succeed
b) I work very hard and usually succeed
c) I work at things that come easily and produce immediate rewards
d) I give up at the first obstacle

7. When it comes to solving problems
a) I use my own resources, logic, intuition and imagination until I find a solution
b) I research the problem and usually arrive at a solution
c) I seek the help of others for solutions
d) I'm not very good at solving problems

8. Where honesty and integrity are concerned
a) I uphold both at all costs
b) I use my judgment and try to be the best person I can whenever possible
c) I frequently bend the rules and compromise my integrity
d) I don't really have a code of behavior for myself

9. When I find myself in a less than ideal situation
a) I am always willing to compromise to make the best of a situation
b) I hold on to my ideals until I see that a compromise is the only way
c) I find it hard to compromise and do so reluctantly
d) I do not compromise under any circumstances

Do You Have What It Takes?

10. When life becomes difficult
a) I try to see the humor in it and keep a balanced perspective
b) I try to solve my problem but not always with the best attitude
c) I sink into a bad mood for a while but usually manage to overcome the problem
d) I get depressed and discouraged and usually give up

To score yourself to see if you have what it takes to become an English teacher in Japan, give yourself 3 points for every (a), 2 points for every (b), 1 point for every (c), and zero for every (d).

Bonus Points
a) I already have a job awaiting me in Japan: 10 points
b) I speak Japanese: 10 points
c) I have relatives or friends living in Japan: 5 points
d) I have traveled extensively in other foreign countries: 3 points

If you scored
More than 25 – Ganbatte! You have what it takes!

21-25 – You may encounter some difficulty, but you will probably succeed.

10-20 – Take a look at your weak areas and get yourself prepared for the challenge.

Less than 10 – Don't even think about it.

The Basic Criteria
At a minimum, the following ten assets and attributes are essential for a successful and rewarding experience in Japan: a college education, adequate finances, good physical health, courage, adaptability, perseverance, resourcefulness, integrity, a willingness to compromise, and a sense of humor. Each attribute plays a crucial role in your ability to thrive and succeed in such unfamiliar and competitive surroundings.

College Education
Although it is possible to find employment as an English teacher in Japan without a degree in English, your probabilities increase exponentially if you have one. A degree of any kind is better than none at all, and the best credential is a BA or better in English with an ESL

certificate. Many employers specifically require that a job candidate meet these criteria, and those employers who do not insist upon it are still more likely to hire those individuals who do. Of course, many individuals without college degrees earn a perfectly good living by providing private English lessons to children, businessmen and housewives. But they are the exception to the rule, and these types of teachers typically have some other means of staying in the country, such as a spouse with a work visa. In general however, freelancing of this kind does not meet the government standards for procuring and maintaining a work visa in Japan. To obtain a work visa, you must include your original college degree (not a photocopy) in your documentation when you apply for it at the Japanese Embassy. The bottom line is: If you want to get hired by a reputable English conversation school, a large corporation, a junior high or high school, stay in school yourself and get your diploma before you head for Japan.

Adequate Finances
By now you've probably heard how expensive it is to live in Japan: $100 watermelons, $70 taxi rides, $20 movie tickets, $6 cups of coffee. Sadly, it's all true. The good news is there's a practical way around it. "When in Rome…" The secret to making the most of your yen is to eat, sleep, play and live Japanese style. Don't drink coffee, don't ride in taxis, don't go to the movies, and don't buy imported commodities. Instead, drink green tea (it packs just as potent a punch as coffee), and take the train or the subway to your appointments. For entertainment, take a taste tour of the food markets located in the basements of large department stores, enjoy a stroll in a temple garden at twilight, or a walk through the trendy shopping streets of Harajuku and the cultural patchwork of Yoyogi Park on Sunday afternoon. For your meals, eat at budget establishments such as stand up *ramen* bars, *yakitori* shops, and *kaitenzushi*; or cook at home if you have a kitchen. If you eat like the natives do, which means lots of rice, vegetables, tofu, and fish, not only will it help you stay within your budget, but you're also more likely to get the full effect from your Japan experience. Bottom line: unless you have already secured a job and a place to live, don't go to Japan with anything less than $3500 cash, more if you can manage it. And do all you can to make it last until you bank your first paycheck.

There's a very helpful website called Price Check Tokyo **www.pricechecktokyo.com** that will give you a good idea of the current cost of everyday commodities such as bread, toothpaste, coffee, gasoline, newspapers, and Internet access in the Tokyo metropolitan area.

Good Health and Stamina

Japan has one of the most advanced and efficient public transit systems of any nation on the planet, but automobiles are ridiculously expensive, and therefore you will probably have to rely on the railway system for the daily task of traveling from home to work and back. This often requires a great deal of walking to and from the train stations, in all kinds of weather. Japan is hot, humid and rainy in the summer, and depending on where you are, it is cold and sometimes even snows in the winter. So, unless you have a generous salary for an apartment in an ideal location, and an expense account for taxi fare or the use of a personal car, you'd best be in good physical shape for walking or bicycling at least part of the way wherever you go. Bicycles are quite common and affordable in Japan, and provide good basic transportation for errands and commuting to and from the train station. Therefore, the ability to walk or bicycle to and from your local destinations is a minimum requirement. And, of course, if you hope to enjoy any amount of recreational travel, good physical stamina and vigor are a must.

Japan also has an excellent health care system, with fairly adequate social and cultural support for foreigners. Be advised however, when it comes to health, the Japanese ideology differs significantly from western medical practices, and the challenge of explaining one's symptoms and figuring out exactly what ailment you have and what kind of drugs a doctor has prescribed can be somewhat bewildering. There are a limited number of clinics in the metropolitan areas with native English-speaking doctors who specialize in treating foreigners, but they are few and far between. And those individuals with ongoing health conditions that require medications such as insulin, thyroid supplements, antidepressants, and even women who take oral contraceptives, would be well advised to make special arrangements for them in advance.

Courage

Japan is one of the safest and most culturally advanced civilizations on earth, and English truly is its second language. But for a first-time visitor, Japan can be like nothing you ever imagined. Even the most innocuous and commonplace occurrences can be profoundly disturbing if you're unprepared for the experience. Here are some examples:

The transit system in Tokyo is massive and labyrinthian. It is jam-packed to capacity and beyond at rush hour every day, with millions of bustling businessmen and women scurrying to their offices. Witnessing the debarkation of the express train at Shinjuku Station is one of the most harrowing experiences on earth. It's a veritable *tsunami* of humanity, most of them Japanese businessmen dressed in blue suits and white dress shirts, all of one mind: getting to work on time. In their haste, they sweep across the train platform and down the stairs, barreling over anything and anyone in their path. If you're lucky, you won't have to join that rat race, but you've gotta see it, at least once.

Getting around in Japan can be tricky too. Many of the signs and markers in the train stations and along the city streets are written exclusively in Japanese, a language whose pictograph alphabet is impossible to look up in a dictionary without some basic knowledge of it. So, until you learn how to interpret directions and navigate your way around the city, you may frequently end up without a clue where you are, where you're going or how to get back home again.

And, with the exception of bars and taxis, almost everything shuts down well before midnight. So it would not be uncommon to miss the last train and find yourself in some remote part of the city after hours, with no way to get home save a $100 taxi ride, and nary an English speaker in sight to help you tell the driver how to get you there. Always check the train schedules and make sure you're at the station in time to catch the last one.

Also, you might be hard at work in a high rise building when Mother Nature begins to shake, rattle and roll. Japan is an archipelago of volcanic islands, and has hundreds of earthquakes every year, albeit most of them harmless.

But they are a common occurrence, and you would be wise to brush up on basic safety procedures in the event that one strikes while you are there.

As for crime, despite what you may have heard about the dark underworld of Japan's *yakuza*, among regular folk, bicycle and umbrella theft is about as bad as it gets. That's not to say that crime doesn't happen, but if you practice common sense and don't invite trouble, there's little to worry about.

Adaptability

Japan is a land of unique lifestyles and customs. Undoubtedly, most westerners are familiar with the Japanese practice of removing shoes at the door, eating raw fish, and driving on the left-hand side of the road. But it doesn't end there. The Japanese people have a highly specific code of behavior and etiquette for every event, from birth celebrations to funerals, and everything else in between. Therefore, it is not only possible, but highly likely that an unwitting foreigner will commit a faux pas at almost every turn. Over time, however, with an eye for nuance and an ability to adapt, you can learn how to behave appropriately in most every situation.

And then there are the furnishings and paraphernalia of everyday life. Things like chopsticks, *futon* beds, *furo* baths, squat toilets, on-demand water heaters, and *kotatsu* tables with foot warmers underneath. In public places, there are talking vehicles, automatic taxi door openers, color-coded telephones, *pachinko* parlors, love hotels, and vending machines that dispense everything from batteries to kilos of rice. Not to mention a language that requires *three* alphabets.

But, if you keep an open mind and a willingness to adapt to your surroundings, chances are you'll survive quite nicely.

Perseverance

After a long day of trudging from interview to interview, and looking at one apartment after another, you may find yourself flagging, if not ready to turn tail and flee back to the comfort and familiarity of home. Here is where perseverance pays off and is perhaps the most important element of your quest. In order to succeed, it is imperative that you do your research, talk to the locals, make your phone calls, buy your newspapers, and follow *every single lead*, no matter how remote or how small. Do this every day, without fail. Keep detailed notes, make yourself a list of all the possibilities you discovered throughout the day: every job opportunity, every agency, every reference, and every available apartment. At the end of each day, take some quiet time to relax and develop a game plan for how you're going to follow up on them all tomorrow. And then get up the next day and do it all over again until you succeed.

Resourcefulness

Finding a job and a place to live in Japan requires a well-rounded repertoire of resources. This may include the prospects you turned up in your research before you left home, as well as any opportunities you may have discovered on location in Japan. The best resources are personal contacts and references, guidebooks, newspapers, local residents, and especially the Internet. The secret lies in how fully you explore and utilize those resources. Therefore, it is essential that you do your homework, keep very thorough and organized notes, follow up on every lead, and don't overlook any possibility.

Integrity

One of the defining qualities of the Japanese people is their integrity. Qualities such as a strong work ethic, pride in workmanship, team effort, and deeply felt shame in the face of failure are inherent to the culture. And for such a densely populated nation, there is remarkably little drug abuse, petty crime, and vagrancy. Not that Japan doesn't have its share of such problems; and granted the newspaper headlines sensationalize bizarre but isolated incidents and scandalous tales of corruption in high places. But on a personal level, in everyday life among the common folk, honor and integrity are the gold standard. Therefore, it is recommended that you conduct yourself with the highest code of behavior and ethics at all times. It will serve you well and keep you out of trouble.

Willingness to Compromise

While you're planning your move to Japan, it's easy to dream in Technicolor: the perfect job, the perfect apartment, the perfect experience. Yet, no matter how carefully you plan and prepare, there will always be those elements that don't meet your expectations. Early on, before you've assimilated the culture and explored the opportunities that await you there, it may be tempting to hold on to that unwavering paragon. However, if you are lucky enough to be offered a pleasant job that meets your basic living expenses with a little disposable income left over for fun, by all means, take it. If you find an affordable apartment that feels homey and livable, go for it. Remember, once you're settled and employed, you can always trade up.

A Sense of Humor

Despite its charm, sophistication and refinement, Japan can also be exhausting, bewildering, infuriating, overwhelming, and downright absurd at times. And when the travails and tribulations of your day frazzle your last nerve, sometimes the only antidote is a sense of humor. So, if you didn't travel to Japan with a companion, find yourself a buddy to swap stories with and have a laugh at day's end. It will help to put the whole crazy circus into perspective, and will provide an outlet for your frustrations, as well as a high-five for your triumphs. English-speaking ex-pats are everywhere in Japan, and most are more than happy to meet up with a kindred spirit. In the beginning, or anytime thereafter for that matter, don't hesitate to strike up a conversation on the train, in a pub, a shop, or even on the street. You have nothing to lose, and may gain a mentor and compatriot for the effort.

Onward and Upward

Now that you've heard all the daunting details and decided that you're made of the "right stuff" to become an English teacher in Japan, proceed to the next chapter to discover what opportunities await you there. If you possess all or most of the assets outlined here, you're certain to find an abundant market for your skills and qualifications.

Notes:

Do You Have What It Takes?

The Contemporary Job Market

For English teachers in Japan, the decade of the 1980's and early 1990's, nostalgically referred to as the "Bubble Years," was a golden era in the Japanese economy. The Nikei soared, the yen held strong on the world currency market, productivity was up, and the pocketbooks of its citizens were fat with disposable income to spend on English lessons. But that impossibly inflated bubble burst in the mid 1990's, and the resulting economic downturn has affected the job market accordingly, making it somewhat more challenging for foreign teachers seeking employment there. Nevertheless, Japan consistently maintains a vigorous and competitive position on the global stage, and its citizens still recognize the value of studying English, perhaps now more than ever.

Who Studies English?

Most Japanese children begin studying English in the sixth grade, some even sooner; and they continue to do so throughout the rest of their academic curriculum. Many students also enroll in *juku*, English cram schools, which they attend early in the morning before their regular school day begins, or in the afternoons after school. Some Japanese families enroll their toddlers in special English programs to give them the earliest possible exposure to the language. Thousands of ambitious Japanese businessmen and women attend conversation salons in the evenings with the goal of improving their language skills to give them an edge in their careers. Large corporations employ English teachers to conduct private on-site classes for their executives, and countless individuals hire private tutors for lessons in their homes or in cafes and coffee shops to help them improve their English skills. So, who studies English in Japan? Just about everybody.

How Abundant are Job Opportunities in Japan?

On any given Monday, at any time of the year, a job seeker can expect to find five to seven pages of classified ads in the *Japan Times*, offering dozens of opportunities for English instructors to teach in schools, conversation salons, private companies, and personal lessons. While most of these jobs are located somewhere in the Tokyo metropolitan area, there are also a limited number of listings for other cities and regions in Japan. In all the metropolitan areas, the larger English language institutions are always looking for instructors. Their ads appear weekly in the Monday classifieds, side by side with those of smaller schools and companies that can sometimes offer more intimate and unique teaching opportunities.

In addition to the traditional method of finding work through the classified ads, the Internet is a growing resource for teaching opportunities in Japan. A simple keyword search using "jobs Japan" or "English teacher Japan" will yield dozens of web sites that offer an abundant variety of job listings for English teachers. (More about the Internet in Chapter Three.)

How Much Can One Expect to Earn Teaching English in Japan?

While salaries vary from time to time and place to place, the full-time entry-level salary starts at around ¥250,000 per month (the minimum allowed for a work visa). For college level teachers, private corporate classes, or for management positions, salaries can increase to ¥350,000 to ¥500,000 or even more per month. And for part time work, depending on a teacher's qualifications, and the type of job, hourly wages range anywhere from ¥2,000 to ¥10,000 or more.

How does this translate into U.S. dollars? Although the currency exchange rate between the U.S. and Japan rises and dips dramatically from time to time, sometimes falling below ¥100 to the dollar, sometimes rising above ¥200, over the past decade it has remained somewhere in the neighborhood of ¥125 to the dollar. Using that as an average, here's the math: For a teacher earning ¥2,000 per hour at ¥125 to the dollar, that comes to $16 per hour. At ¥10,000 per hour, a teacher earns an hourly rate of $80. For part-time work the pay usually falls somewhere in between.

For a full time salaried teacher working 25 to 40 hours per week, ¥250,000 per month comes out to about $2000 per month. At the upper end of the teaching salary range, ¥500,000 equals $4000 per month. Most reputable schools and companies offer paid vacations and holidays, a rail pass, a yearly bonus equal to a month's salary, and sometimes a contract-signing bonus. Some jobs also include visa sponsorship, health insurance, an apartment, and even round trip airfare.

Income Taxes

Japan has an income tax system quite similar to that of the U.S., and all workers earning an income in Japan, even foreigners, are required to pay taxes. Income tax is withheld at both the national and local level, and there are three separate tax rates for foreign workers based on their length of residency in Japan. The tax year runs from January 1 to December 31, and taxes are due between February 16 and March 15 of the following year. Much the same as in the U.S., deductions are allowed for any expenses incurred in the process of earning income. However, salaried workers are not typically required to submit a return, because taxes are deducted from their paychecks throughout the year. In December, a year-end adjustment is made to compensate for any excesses or deficit in the year's with-holding. And when a foreign worker with an annual income of more than ¥350,000 leaves Japan permanently, a final tax return must be filed and the taxes paid before departure.

Beyond the Paycheck

Opportunities for earning extra money in Japan are also abundant. If you happen to be blessed with great looks, there's always modeling. For those with a melodic speaking voice, there's voice-over work for commercial videotapes and television ads. And for the musically inclined, there's a constant demand for entertainment in nightclubs and other venues. And of course, every smart *Eigo no sensei* has a private student or two on the side to help make ends meet and provide a little extra spending money.

The Bottom Line

While these figures and averages fluctuate according to the economy, they have remained fairly consistent over the past decade and can be trusted as a reliable index for evaluating your opportunities and prospects. Of course, with the cost of living in Japan, these pay rates are not likely to make you wealthy overnight, but the average salary is usually more than enough to cover basic living expenses for a thrifty and conscientious spender living a modest Japanese lifestyle. By maximizing their earning potential and minimizing their overhead, many resourceful teachers even manage to put aside a tidy sum to take home with them. Bonuses and paid vacations are great for excursions to other regions of Japan, for trips home to visit family and friends, and for travel to other Asian countries. Teaching English in Japan is an excellent way to subsidize an Asian adventure.

Notes:

Making the Move

I cannot emphasize strongly enough the importance of adequate preparation before embarking on your odyssey to work in Japan. Of course, nothing can fully prepare you for the culture shock that awaits you at Narita Airport, but the more you familiarize yourself beforehand with the language, the customs, the cuisine, the culture, the history, the geography, the economy, and the currency exchange, the less likely you are to be rendered catatonic after an all-night plane flight; and the more likely you are to successfully navigate your way to your first night's lodgings and beyond.

Ten Must Do's Before Making Your Move to Japan

Make sure that your passport is valid for at least a year.

The last thing you'd want to have to do is figure out how to renew your passport from Japan while you're still trying to figure out how to find your way home from the train station after work every night. You can apply for a passport at over 4,500 passport acceptance facilities including Federal, state and probate courts, post offices, libraries and county and municipal offices. The 13 official U.S. passport agencies are usually reserved for urgent departures and require an appointment. The Department of State provides complete information on the application process and a list of local passport facilities throughout the U.S. at **http://travel.state.gov/passport_services.html**

To apply for a passport you will need an application form (available to print out from the website), an official birth certificate or proof of citizenship, a driver's license or other ID, two passport photos, a check for $45 to "Passport Services" and another $15 check for the clerk at the passport facility. Once the application has been submitted, your passport will arrive by mail in about six weeks. For those in need of a passport in less than six weeks, for an additional $35, a passport may be issued in seven to ten days at a passport agency or via overnight mail. If you have an expired passport that is less than 15 years old, is undamaged and was issued to you after age 16 under your present name, it may be renewed by mail. Instructions for renewing a passport are also available online.

Check the latest vaccination requirements.
Japan is a wondrously advanced nation, and vaccinations are not typically required. But you never know. Vaccinations can also be especially important if you plan to travel from Japan to other Asian destinations. Make a list of any countries you might visit and check the vaccination requirements for those countries as well. The National Center for Infectious Diseases website contains comprehensive and up-to-date information on vaccination requirements and precautions for many worldwide destinations. **www.cdc.gov/travel/vaccinat.htm** For basic protection in Japan, the Center recommends vaccinations for Hepatitis A and B, Typhoid, Rabies, Tetanus-Diphtheria, Measles, Polio, and for Japanese Encephalitis if you plan to spend more than four weeks in a rural area.

Buy a round trip ticket.
Round trip airfare is recommended for a number of reasons. First, you may not be allowed entry into Japan on a 90-day landing permit (tourist visa) with a one-way plane ticket. And unless you're among the small percentage of individuals who manage to procure a work visa before moving to Japan, you'll have to start out with a tourist visa, and upgrade to a work visa once you've found a job, and you will have to travel to a Japanese Consulate or Embassy outside Japan to get it. (More about that in the section on Immigration). A good suggestion is to buy a round trip ticket to Seoul, with an extended stopover in Tokyo. Once you've found a job, use the Tokyo-Seoul-Tokyo segment of the ticket to go to South Korea to get your work visa. Airline tickets purchased in Japan are considerably more expensive than purchasing from within the U.S. or through online ticket agents. Some airlines offer multi-segmented tickets with extended stopovers good for up to a year.

Get yourself connected with contacts in Japan.

When relocating to Japan to seek employment and a place to live, one of the most valuable assets you can have is a personal connection with someone who is already living there, whether a fellow teacher, or a Japanese citizen. And although it may seem like a distant possibility, the thread of destiny that connects you to Japan may be closer than you realize. Think *Six Degrees of Separation*, and don't overlook even the remotest of prospects: Your next-door neighbor's boyfriend's college roommate, your old high-school classmate with the Japanese mom, that guy from Starbucks who's always reminiscing about his days as an English teacher in Japan, that cute girl whose dad travels to Japan on business, the nice Japanese student who sits next to you in class, the friendly Japanese tourists you happen to meet in the park, or the owner of your favorite sushi bar. And don't be shy. The Japanese can be very open, welcoming people; and the majority of Westerners who live in Japan, or who have lived there, or who have friends who live there, are often quite willing to hook you up if you express a sincere interest in moving to Japan. So keep your eyes and ears open for likely allies.

Study the language.

You'll need it. And not just a couple of touristy phrases. Although an impressive number of Japanese citizens speak English, many still do not. This is especially true of the millions of people who are employed in some of the most common of domestic activities for everyday interaction, such as shopkeepers, waiters, postal workers, receptionists, barbers, taxi drivers, and deliverymen. While many of these individuals may have studied English throughout their academic years, they don't often get a chance to use it on a daily basis. Therefore it is essential for you to learn the basics and meet them halfway when it comes to handling money, shopping for groceries and household items, purchasing tickets and stamps, ordering from a menu, finding your way around town, and comprehending instructions.

The Japanese language is made up of three separate alphabets: *Kanji* (the brush-stroke characters used to depict objects and to convey abstract concepts), *Hiragana* (the shorthand-looking characters used to denote tense and grammar) and *Katakana* (the angular characters used to write foreign words). Go to a good bookstore, get yourself a basic Hiragana / Katakana primer and learn those characters first. They will serve you well until you begin to recognize the kanji characters that you're exposed to everyday in Japan. You can also order Japanese language books online on the Amazon.com website **www.amazon.com** using the keywords "Japanese language."

Another way to learn the language is to study Japanese online. A website called Find Tutorials **www.findtutorials.com** offers links to hundreds of web sites on almost every subject imaginable, including language lessons in nearly every language. The Japanese page contains a list of a dozen or so web sites that offer basic Japanese lessons. Here's a tip for making sure you study on a daily basis: Put a link to the lesson page on the start up menu of your computer. It will upload automatically and remind you to study each day when you turn on your computer. To do this in Microsoft Windows, copy the website URL of the online lesson page and paste it into the startup file in C:\WINDOWS\Start Menu\Programs\StartUp.

If you happen to be ambitious enough to learn to read a few kanji characters before you go, the most useful ones would be the kanji for North, South, East, and West; Up, Down, In, and Out; Push and Pull; Beef, Chicken, Pork, Fish, Egg and Vegetable, and the numbers from one to ten, as well as the characters for one hundred and one thousand. And if you're feeling particularly motivated, it's worthwhile to learn to write your own name in katakana. If you can manage to get a good grasp of these few things, you'll be way ahead of the game.

And do invest in a good pocket-sized Japanese dictionary before you leave. Imported books can be very pricey in Japan. When choosing a dictionary, in addition to the contents, pay close attention to how the spine of the book is stitched. You'll be using it dozens of times throughout the day, and some of the dictionaries currently available, especially the thicker ones, tend to come unglued and the pages fall out. The best ones are soft and flexible with very thin pages and vinyl covers.

Another very useful Japanese language book is Todd and Erika Geers' *Making Out in Japanese*. This little phrasebook contains everyday expressions that you won't find in dictionaries and textbooks; phrases to help you with casual chatting, handling yourself with conflicts, and even the language of romance.

Just for starters, here are a few essential phrases to practice before you go:

O-hayo-gozaimasu – Good morning

Kon-nichi-wa – Hello (in the daytime)

Kon-ban-wa – Good evening

O-yasumi-nasai – Good night

Hajime-mashite – Nice to meet you

Gomen-nasai – I'm sorry

Su-re-shimasu – Pardon me

Kudasai – Please

Arigato – Thank you

Do-itashi-mashite – You're welcome

Sumi-masen – Attention please

Dozo – Be my guest, After you, or Please accept what I offer

Itadakimasu- A before meal thank you

Go-shi-so-sama – An after meal thank you

O-tsukari-sama-deshita – We did it! Time to celebrate!

Study Japan's history, culture, economics, customs, and current events.

Japan is a culture unlike any other on earth. It is a complex composite of nuance and nationalism, a paradox of ancient tradition and futuristic vision, a juxtaposition of the elegant and the rustic, an equipoise of cacophony and serenity, a polarity of toil and *joie de vivre*. Studying the culture beforehand will give you invaluable insight into those elements that are not readily understandable to outsiders. The more you know, the less likely you are to commit an unforgivable blunder;

and the more likely you are to conduct yourself with tact and grace in unfamiliar situations. Even a little bit goes a long way. There are dozens of excellent texts on these subjects, but my personal favorites are: *Passport's Japan Almanac* by Boye De Mente (currently out of print but still available through used book dealers on the Internet); *The Chrysanthemum and the Sword* by Ruth Benedict; and for a lighter perspective, *Dave Barry Does Japan* is right on the mark. You can locate these and other texts (including the out-of-print titles) online on the Amazon.com website **www.amazon.com**

Research employment opportunities from home and schedule your first job interviews before you leave.
The Internet is now the quintessential resource for this endeavor, and will yield an abundance of resource sites and job opportunities with a simple keyword search. However the bewildering number of web sites and the dozens of jobs posted on each one can leave you feeling a little dizzy. When searching for resources and opportunities online, it is important to get all your maps and materials organized. Keep detailed notes, print out copies of all promising leads, set up links and bookmarks on your web browser, and create shortcuts to your resume and cover letter for immediate e-mail responses to prospective employers. The more diligent and organized you are, the more effective your search results will be. (More about using the Internet in Chapter Three.)

If you can get your hands on a recent copy of the *Japan Times* classified section, it is also an excellent job-hunting resource. However, only the Monday edition features the employment classifieds. If someone you know is traveling to Japan you might ask them to bring back a copy for you, or you can request an overseas subscription by e-mail to **overseas@japantimes.co.jp**. You can also call the *Japan Times* Subscription Department in Tokyo at (03) 3453-4350. However, you may find an overseas subscription quite costly. The *Japan Times* has a website too. **www.japantimes.co.jp** But don't be fooled by the link to the classified ads. They are not available for viewing online. The link takes you to a page containing only the advertising rates. But you can contact the subscription department online and take the opportunity to read up on the latest news from Japan while you're there.

Pack only the essentials.

Unless you can afford the emperor's ransom it costs to have a limo waiting for you when you arrive, you're going to have to lug all your worldly possessions from the airport to wherever you'll be staying for the first few days. So definitely get some luggage with wheels, and only pack what you can't live without. Watch the weather reports to see what kind of clothes would be most suitable for the time of your arrival and pack accordingly. Also, remember that items such as toiletries, cosmetics, and other sundries, albeit pricey, are readily available. In fact, shopping is a national pastime in Japan, and the array of merchandise is dazzling. You will even see many familiar American brand-name products, however, you will no doubt find their domestic counterparts comparable in quality but considerably more affordable. Remember however, that the physical stature of the Japanese tends to be somewhat smaller than average, so if you're a "Big & Tall" size, don't count on finding clothes to fit you right off the rack. In which case, a little extra packing may be justified. (More on what to take with you in Chapter Ten.)

**Prepare yourself a care package in
advance to send via surface mail.**

In a sturdy box, pack up a few treasures you'd like to have once you've set up house in Japan. It might be some extra clothing for the upcoming season, a few of your favorite books, some comfort foods such as canned soup, peanut butter, macaroni and cheese, or Jello; a few framed photographs of family and friends, or even a favorite teddy bear. These nostalgic items will make your new surroundings feel more like home when you miss it most. Once you've got a permanent address, ask a trusted friend or family member to ship your package to you. Surface mail to Japan takes about six weeks. But don't be surprised when your box arrives with its contents meticulously but conspicuously repacked. The Japanese customs office is very strict and very thorough. The following web page, maintained by the Japanese government's Ministry of Finance, contains specific information on which items are restricted or prohibited.
www.mof.go.jp/~customs/fvisit-e.htm Tokyo's Narita Airport lists its guidelines and restrictions at **www.narita-airport-customs.go.jp/** In the U.S., the Department of State also provides information on Japan travel and customs at this web address:

http://travel.state.gov/japan.html Among the list of items prohibited by Japanese customs are: firearms and ammunition, smoking paraphernalia, pornographic materials, narcotics, over-the-counter medications that contain stimulants (including Tylenol Cold, Nyquil, Nyquil Liquicaps, Actifed, Sudafed, Advil Cold & Sinus, Dristan Cold "No Drowsiness," Dristan Sinus, Drixoral Sinus, Vicks Inhaler, and Lomotil). Restricted items include plants and animals (subject to inspection and approval), non-prescription medications (no more than a two months' supply), cosmetics (no more than 24 pieces), and weapons such as swords and hunting guns (permit required). The website also contains a list of limits on duty free goods including alcoholic beverages (three bottles), cigars (100), cigarettes (400), and perfume (two ounces). Any goods in excess of these limits are subject to duty fees.

Get yourself psyched up for the lifestyle change.

Start eating, living and thinking Japanese. Take your shoes off when you walk in the door. Learn the names of all the different kinds of Japanese foods and beverages and how to prepare some of them. Pay attention to Japanese events in the daily news. Learn the names of key politicians, athletes and celebrities. Rent Japanese movies on video. (Juzo Itami's *Tampopo* is a great little movie, as are his numerous other films.) Read Japanese literature. (*Kitchen* by Banana Yoshimoto is a *wonderful* place to start; as is the Japanese classic *Botchan* by Natsume Soseki, Japan's most beloved author). Incorporating a Japanese lifestyle into your everyday life in the months and weeks before you travel will add to the excitement and focus of your goal; and every little thing you do to prepare yourself will enhance your ability to adapt and succeed in Japan.

The Best Time To Go

Since there are teaching opportunities to be had every day in Japan, there really is no "best" time to go. However certain times are more or less favorable than others, depending on the area in which you plan to settle, what season you arrive, and what kind establishment you choose to work for.

Throughout the year, in corporate as well as academic venues, the Japanese people celebrate a series of holidays, during which many, if not most businesses and schools are closed. Needless to say, if you arrive during any of these holiday seasons, you may not find anyone available to interview and hire you, and you will therefore be stuck spending your finite resources on meals and lodgings until normal business resumes. The three major holiday seasons are:

Oshogatsu – The Japanese New Year Holiday, December 25 - January 5
During this time, the Japanese people celebrate the end of their work year with corporate parties, and commemorate the beginning of the New Year with family gatherings, visits to shrines and temples, special foods, gifts and festivals. For most schools and companies, regular business activities are suspended during this holiday season.

Golden Week, April 29 - May 5
This season of celebration is actually a combination of several holidays, including April 29 - former Emperor Hirohito's Birthday (now known as Greenery Day); May 3 – Japan's Constitution Day; and May 5 - Childrens' Day. During this week in early Spring, most schools and businesses are closed, and many people take the opportunity to travel. So not only is business suspended, but planes, trains and hotels are fully booked.

Obon – the Japanese Festival of the Dead, August 10 - August 15
Although observance of this holiday season is slightly less pervasive than New Year's and Golden Week, it is a time of many festivals and widespread travel. Following an ancient tradition, the season celebrates the mythical return of the spirits of the departed to the land of the living. On August 13, the Japanese people visit the graves of their ancestors, and on the 15th, special foods are prepared, with places set at the table for departed relatives. The streets and parks are decorated with strings of colorful paper lanterns to mark the path home for deceased loved ones, and in the evenings, special dances called bon odori are performed in temple gardens and public parks. It's a lovely celebration, however it does affect day-to-day business.

Other Holidays in Japan:
January 15 – **Coming of Age Day**
Honors young adults turning 20 years old.

February 11 – **Foundation Day**
Celebrates Japan's first Emperor Jimmu (660 B.C.)

March 22 /23 – **Vernal Equinox**
First Day of Spring

September 15 – **Day for the Aged**
Honors Japan's elderly population.

September 23 – **Autumnal Equinox**
First Day of Autumn

October 10 – **Sports Day**
Celebrates health and physical fitness

November 3 – **Culture Day**
Celebrates Japan's culture and history

November 23 – **Labor Day**
Honors Japan's workforce

An Insider's Secret
Although the major holiday seasons in Japan are not optimal for traveling and seeking employment, many foreign teachers choose to terminate their employment and leave the country around those times. So, during the holiday seasons, there may be more vacancies for teachers. Thus timing your arrival a few weeks before a major holiday may optimize your chances of getting hired.

The School Year in Japan
The academic year in Japan begins in March, so if you hope to find work in a school, it would be wise to seek employment in the late winter months just before the new school year begins. Be forewarned however that February is the least temperate time of year, so be prepared to find a bleak landscape awaiting. But don't be discouraged.

You'll be duly rewarded in a matter of weeks, when the entire country bursts into bloom for *ohanami*, the cherry blossom season. It's pure magic.

The Seasons and Climates of Japan

Japan is a land of many climates, because the islands are spread over so many geographic latitudes, from the sub-arctic island of Hokkaido, to the tropical locale of Okinawa. In the north, Hokkaido and upper Honshu have deep, frigid winters, brisk and breezy springs, chilly autumns, and short summers. Although the mountainous central region of Honshu has an alpine climate, the coastal regions of southern Honshu, and the islands of Shikoku and Kyushu are much more temperate. Winters are milder, with only occasional snow; springs are cool and picturesque, especially during the cherry blossom season, summers can be muggy and humid with temperatures occasionally reaching 100 degrees, and the autumns are crisp and clear. And then there's the rainy season, a separate season unto itself, which begins in late May and lasts until mid-July. Typhoons are also common during the late summer and early fall months. And in addition to the characteristics of each season, the intensely urban areas create a climate of their own by generating heat, light, noise and atmospheric pollution. The city skies are often bleak when the surrounding countryside is otherwise clear, and the starlit beauty of the night sky is frequently eclipsed by the bright city lights. One other important factor to remember: Japan does not observe Daylight Savings Time, so the sun rises quite early in the summer months.

Mapping Out a Timeline

Once you've decided when you want to arrive in Japan, a timeline will help you to prepare so you can wrap up all the details on schedule for your departure. Many of your preparations such as passports, college transcripts, etc. will require several weeks of processing time. Other tasks such as doing research, updating your resume, preparing your surface mail package, etc. will take lots of your personal time. So the more you accomplish early on, the less you'll have left to do in a rush at the last minute. The best way to begin is with a thorough checklist.

One Year Out

Many of the tasks you will need to complete for a successful move to Japan require many months of advance preparation. Once the idea of going is firmly fixed in your mind, it's never too early to start the process. General research can begin as early as a year or more before your target departure date.

Start saving money – The sooner you begin saving money, the more financial resources you will have available to get started in Japan. Unless your living accommodations await you already, $3500 to $5000 is the minimum recommendation to tide you over while you search for an apartment and wait for your first paycheck. Of course you will also have expenses at home before you embark on your journey, such as plane fare, passport fees, and travel supplies.

Begin studying Japanese language, history, culture, and current events – By studying Japanese for a few minutes every day, you will be able to learn the basic elements of the written and spoken language. Of course a language is best assimilated with practical application in everyday life, so you will also benefit by using what you've learned in real-life situations. So find a Japanese tutor or study buddy to help you hone your speaking skills. Japanese restaurants and businesses are also a good place to practice. Many cities have Japanese-owned establishments with native-speaking employees. Don't be shy. Give it a try.

Meanwhile, when choosing recreational reading material, opt for contemporary Japanese fiction and books on Japanese culture. When renting movies, head for the foreign film section and pick up a subtitled Japanese video instead. And when cooking at home or dining out, go Japanese. Every little bit counts.

If your finances permit, begin watching the currency markets for the best value on exchange rates – Even a small dip in the value of the yen can add up to significant savings when you're purchasing large quantities. The Internet is the perfect resource for following the currency market. Some experts recommend buying yen once you're in Japan because the domestic currency exchange rates there tend to be less expensive than buying yen outside Japan. However, due to certain economic events and conditions, there are times when the value of the yen falls dramatically over a period of weeks or months. So it never hurts to keep an eye on the market and take advantage of an opportunity to save yourself a few bucks. It is also possible to convert your dollars directly in to travelers' checks in yen if you happen to find an opportunity to buy yen at an especially low exchange rate. Discuss this option with your banker.

Six Months Out

During this time, continue your studies of Japanese language and culture, and begin studying the job market. Consider the kind of atmosphere in which you would like to work, and familiarize yourself with the various regions of Japan to determine the area in which you would like to live. Evaluate your temperament and lifestyle preferences carefully. Are you more comfortable in the big city, or do you prefer small town life in more rural surroundings? Do you like working for big corporations, or are you happier in a smaller, more intimate establishment? Do you like the idea of working full time for one company, or would a variety of several part-time jobs be more appealing to you? Each of these factors will play a significant role in your happiness and the success of your venture.

Three Months Out

As your departure date approaches, your tasks will become more clearly defined. At this time, you can research and query specific job opportunities, decide on an exact departure date and begin making plane and lodging reservations.

Research and query job opportunities – In the early stages, long before you're ready to hop on a plane to Japan, you can learn a lot about the job market and the hiring process by responding to ads for English instructors. Pick the best ones, those that offer plane fare, visa sponsorship, and an apartment. Applying for jobs that you're not necessarily prepared to accept can be an excellent way to test your skills and qualifications. It will provide you with an opportunity to interact with Japanese employers, to refine your resume, and to familiarize yourself with specific regions and cities. And who knows? In the process, you may just stumble upon the perfect job, in which case, you can always accelerate your preparations and travel arrangements. (Refer to the next chapter for tips and resources for researching job opportunities via the Internet.)

Research plane fares for the best rates – Again, the Internet is an excellent resource for finding the best rates on airfare. There are dozens of travel web sites such as Travelocity **www.travelocity.com**, Orbitz **www.orbitz.com** and Best Fares **www.bestfares.com** that offer searchable databases of comparative airfare. You can also create a personalized homepage at My Yahoo **http://my.yahoo.com**, which offers a customizable fare watch feature that displays the lowest available airfare at all times. Korean Airlines has competitive rates and seasonal specials to Tokyo and Seoul, which you will probably need when you go to get your work visa. Their round trip tickets are typically valid for up to one year. It is also possible to find very economical charter flights on Korean Air thorough certain travel agencies. Watch the Sunday newspaper for these special fares.

Research initial lodgings – This step is best saved for the time when you've narrowed down your choice of cities in which to live and work. If the job you choose provides living accommodations, luckily you can skip this step. However, if the job does not include living accommodations and you're required to find lodgings on your own, then there's no point in beginning your search for a place to stay until you've determined where you're going to be working or seeking employment. But as soon as that has been decided, begin your search immediately for a place to call home while you look for permanent place to live. The following chapter includes numerous links to Internet web sites through which you can locate and reserve rooms at economical family-style *ryokan* or youth hostels.

Two Months Out

Although some of these tasks can be completed sooner, they should be completed no later than this to assure that your documentation arrives in time for your departure date.

Get your passport in order – Getting a passport by mail typically takes about six weeks. The Department of State Passport Services website provides complete information on obtaining or renewing a passport. **http://travel.state.gov/passport_services.html**

Update your resume and print out at least a dozen copies – A good project for a rainy day or a quiet evening, and one of the little details that you can get out of the way and forget about. The resources section of Chapter Twelve contains tips for composing your resume.

Gather your educational documentation – The more documentation you have, the more smoothly and successfully the hiring process will go. Transcripts, diplomas, certificates, awards, and letters of recommendation are excellent ways to supplement your resume. However, documents such as transcripts and letters of recommendation can require a few weeks to process, so don't wait until the last minute.

One Month Out

Now the real fun begins. This is the time to set your plans in motion, to begin your employment search in earnest and determine how to handle your domestic affairs in your absence. Staying organized, following a checklist and keeping detailed notes is now more important than ever.

Contact prospective employers to set up interviews – Veterans of the job quest in Japan will tell you that the only way to get hired for a job is to apply in person. While this is essentially true, and to be sure, no Japanese employer is going to hire you sight unseen, you can contact prospective employers and set up interviews from home once you have decided on your departure date and purchased your plane ticket. You can send them your resume and photo via e-mail, and keep in contact with them in the interim. That way, when you arrive in Japan, they will already be familiar with you, and you may proceed to the second phase of the interview process.

Begin making arrangements for your personal affairs while you are away – While you're living in Japan, you will need to make arrangements for your mail, your bank account, your credit cards, your house or apartment, and any important family matters such as child support payments, and other financial or personal obligations.

If you're giving up your present address while you're in Japan, you can make arrangements at your local post office for mail to be forwarded to a friend's or relative's address while you're gone. Change of address forms are available online at the U.S. Postal Service website. **www.usps.com**

You will need to talk to your banker to inquire about keeping your dormant accounts open, and you might also inquire about how to make deposits from overseas in the event that you want to bank a few of your hard-earned yen back home. One safe, inexpensive, yet little-known method of sending money home is to buy travelers checks in U.S. dollars in Japan, and mail them along with a deposit slip to your bank via certified mail.

For your credit cards, it's a good idea to notify the bank that issued them that you will be living abroad, and inquire whether any special arrangements need to be made. And be sure to pay off any outstanding balances before you leave. Even the smallest amount left unpaid can reflect negatively on your credit rating. You might also wish to inquire about using your credit card while you're in Japan. Major credit cards are accepted worldwide, but you will probably need to arrange to make your monthly payments from outside the country. Contact your credit card company's customer service department for information.

When arranging for a house sitter, a trusted friend is always the best choice. But even then, you may find that when you're ready to return, your friend is unwilling to vacate your home. As one who's been there myself and heard tales from others, this kind of conflict is much more common than you might imagine. So here's a word to the wise: Make sure the landlord approves your sub-let, and draft up a signed, witnessed agreement with your house sitter that clearly defines the terms and duration of your house sitter's tenancy in your absence, including a clause that covers you in the event you decide to return from Japan sooner than expected.

Give notice at your job – Depending upon your present employer and how long you plan to work in Japan, you may want to opt for taking a leave of absence instead of quitting your job. If you're a valued member of the staff, many employers are willing to grant a leave of absence for up to one year. If you prefer to terminate your employment, it's always an appreciated courtesy to give at least two week's notice.

Two Weeks Out

As your departure date approaches, your plans will start to become reality. This is an increasingly important time for attention to detail, a time to continue to stay organized with your checklist and timeline.

Begin packing your luggage – The best place to begin your packing is with a thorough checklist of all the things you think you'll need when you arrive in Japan. Your list should include clothing, toiletries and grooming products, any special medications you may require, your official papers and documentation, contact information for personal and business correspondence, your Japan contact information, and all your research materials. Avoid the temptation to over pack your luggage however, as you will probably have to lug it at least part of the way through airports and city streets on both ends of your trip. So stick to the essentials and perhaps a few lightweight creature comforts.

Prepare your surface mail package – While you are packing your luggage for the flight to Japan, it's also a good idea to begin assembling your surface mail package at the same time. By preparing the contents of your luggage and your shipping container side by side, you can ask yourself the question, "Will I need this item immediately, or can it wait until I have a permanent address?" This method will help you avoid the tendency to over pack. When you're finished packing the box, seal it up securely and put a blank address label on it. Leave the package, and enough money to cover the shipping fees, with a friend or family member who can mail it to you once you notify them of your permanent address in Japan. Surface mail to Japan takes about six weeks. Of course, if you're willing to spend the extra money to ship it sooner, there are several much faster options.

Make arrangements for any medical needs – The Japanese customs department only allows you to bring a month's supply of prescription drugs into the country, accompanied by a copy of the prescription. So, if you happen to have any kind of health condition that requires regular prescription medication, or you use oral contraceptives, you will need to make arrangements with your doctor for a letter of explanation and a copy of your prescription to take to Japan. Once you're there, you will probably need to find a local physician to monitor your condition and provide you with a Japanese prescription. The larger cities in Japan all have medical facilities with English speaking physicians, and the Japanese counterparts for pharmaceutical medications are readily available.

One Week Out

Pay farewell visits to family and friends – A year is a long time to be away from family and friends. So, no matter how chaotic things get in the days before you leave, take the time to enjoy a heartfelt farewell with your loved ones. You'll be glad you did. The experience will remain with you and sustain you in many ways throughout your stay in Japan.

Finish packing your luggage – Throughout the packing process, no doubt you will also be wearing and using certain things you plan to take with you. During your last week at home, begin adding those last minute items to your luggage.

Three Days Out

Now's the time for the final details and for wrapping up all your domestic affairs. Continue to keep your checklist close at hand and use it to jot down anything that you may have forgotten.

Pay your outstanding bills – In these last few days before you leave, pay all your bills, and if necessary, make arrangements for your utilities to be shut off and your deposits refunded. Because your most recent statement may not reflect everything you owe, you may have to call your utility and credit card companies to verify the full amount of your outstanding balance. Even a small balance left unpaid can negatively impact your credit rating.

Buy traveler's checks – Traveler's checks are always a wise safeguard. Buy them in U.S. dollars and trade them in for yen when you arrive in Japan. You can also buy travelers checks in yen. This could be useful in the event that you've been watching the currency market and bought your yen at an especially low rate in advance.

Get in touch with your contacts in Japan – Call or e-mail your friends and contacts in Japan to let them know when you will be arriving and if they're not meeting you at the airport, make arrangements to rendezvous with them once you're settled.

The Night Before You Leave

Go over your checklist and double-check everything – No matter how thorough you've been in your preparations, chances are you've forgotten something. Going over your checklist one more time will reduce the likelihood that you've overlooked anything important.

Say farewell to close family and friends – Take the time to say your personal goodbyes one last time before you leave. It can be something as simple as a phone call or dropping by for a quick visit to your close friends and family.

Have a nutritious meal, drink lots of water and get a good night's sleep – International travel can be exhausting. To feel your best on the day you leave, it's important to take care of yourself beforehand. A sensible meal at a reasonable hour, and lots of water the night before, will help you maintain your stamina and keep you from getting dehydrated during your flight. And as tempting as it may be to celebrate your departure with a big bon voyage bash, try to avoid partying too heavily the night before you leave. You're going to need all your strength and energy, and especially your wits to navigate your way to your first night's lodgings in Japan.

Notes:

Making the Move

Researching from Home

The Internet is by far the best resource available for researching all aspects of traveling to Japan to become an English teacher. The World Wide Web offers hundreds of web sites for job opportunities, lodging, travel arrangements, passports and visa information, general advice and survival tips, as well as first-person narratives by people who have successfully navigated their way through the entire Japan experience.

However, the process of navigating the Internet and sifting through the bounty of information can be tricky, if not downright bewildering, just by the mere volume of it; not to mention trying to choose from such a vast array of options. And while the list of web sites presented here in no way represents the whole of it, the links I've selected are maintained by reliable, well-established organizations and businesses whose web sites are likely to still be online by the time you read this. Their highly detailed and informative sites will help you immensely in your quest to live and work in Japan.

Bear in mind however, that the World Wide Web is changing every minute of every day; and at this very moment, new web sites are being created, while others are disappearing. Therefore, a keyword search could yield some newly created sites, while some listed here may have already vanished into cyberspace.

When performing a keyword search, simple words are the most effective, and the more precise and literal, the better. For general employment opportunities, use "jobs Japan" or "teaching English Japan." If you have a preferred region or city, try including that in you keyword search as well, for example "teaching English Kyoto." And for budget lodging in youth hostels or family style inns called *ryokan*, use keywords such as "ryokan Tokyo," or "youth hostel Japan." When your search results appear, investigate the list of web sites not only for their rates, but also for links to other resources. These sites often link to additional job banks, lodging databases, travel bureaus and cultural resources.

Another essential tool to facilitate your search for lodging and employment in Japan is a detailed map of the metropolitan area in which you plan to settle. Tokyo has hundreds of suburbs, and satellite cities, so it's important to have a map handy to get an idea of where jobs and *ryokan* are located in relation to each other and to the transit system. Some of the outlying prefectures (counties) such as Saitama, Chiba or Gunma may require an hour or more of travel by train. And if you plan to look for work in downtown Tokyo, you'd be well advised to choose a *ryokan* that is located somewhere in within the central district rather than one that's too far out in the suburbs.

City maps can be obtained from bookstores, travel agents and motor clubs. Or maps can be purchased online at Maps.com **www.maps.com**. Printable online maps of Japan, Tokyo and especially other smaller cities are surprisingly hard to find. The best I found are on the Discovery.com website. **www.discovery.com** Once you're there, follow these links: Discovery School/For Students/ Social Studies/AtoZ Geography/J for Japan. You'll find a good general map of Japan with zoom links to the Tokyo Metropolitan area. And just for fun, while you're looking for maps, there's a really cool page on the NASA website with a photo of Tokyo taken from the Space Shuttle. **http://earth.jsc.nasa.gov**

Web sites that Contain General Information
Japanorama
www.japanorama.com
A stylish and beautifully designed site with links to hundreds of major resources on every aspect of Japan. The "Japan Info" link is a great place to start your odyssey.

Tokyo Classified
www.tokyoclassified.com
An excellent general resource for all the latest happenings in Tokyo.
Hip and savvy, this online collective will give you the scoop on
entertainment and lifestyle, the latest trends, current events and an
extensive classified section with all the usual features, including help
wanted, apartments, miscellaneous for sale, personals, the works!

Tokyo Globe
www.tokyoglobe.com
This website is packed with news stories and links to Japan's major
newspapers. It has other features too, one of the best being the
Tokyo Survival Guide. It is filled with comprehensive and detailed
information on every aspect of getting settled in Japan. The link to
the Survival Guide is at the very bottom left on the main page.

Japan Information Network
http://jin.jcic.or.jp/
An excellent jumping-off place for all kinds of cultural, historical,
contemporary, statistical, and geographical information.

Escape Artist
www.escapeartist.com/
You'll say Eureka! when you visit this website. Scroll down to the
Country Profiles section and click on the Japan link for a whole new
world of information. Be forewarned however, that you may be lured
to other worldwide destinations.

Embassy World
www.embassyworld.com
An emporium of useful resource links.

Lonely Planet
www.lonelyplanet.com
Good basic travel information. Check out the "Postcards" section for
a hodge-podge of firsthand tips on Japan from veteran travelers.

Rough Guides
www.roughguides.com
A stylish and contemporary resource for general travel information
on any destination.

NTT Japan Window
www.jwindow.net/
Not much in the way of extensive content, but rather a collection of links to other useful sites. Especially helpful in the "Going to Japan" section, is the page containing links to the official web sites for all of Japan's major cities, and many minor ones as well.

Jim Breen's Japanese Page
www.csse.monash.edu.au/~jwb/japanese.html
A mind-boggling and ever-expanding compendium of links to every imaginable resource on all things Japanese. Bookmark this one and start your research here.

Web sites with Firsthand Information on Living and Working in Japan
The JET Alumni Association of Southern California
www.jetaasc.org
An outstanding website with candid and deeply insightful information on every facet of what it's like to live and work in Japan. Unvarnished and intelligently written information that you won't find expressed quite as frankly anywhere else. Although it is intended as a primer for JET participants, the information is universal. This page contains the main menu of links. www.jetaasc.org/php/index.php?index=handbook

Luis Poza's Website
http://poza.net/japan/
Here's a website created by one of my old co-workers from Japan. It's intensely detailed and insightful, with lots of inside information, great suggestions, and words of wisdom from one who definitely knows the ropes. Lots of links to other resources too! Do yourself a favor and don' skip a single page of this website. In fact, this one is so thorough and well written, I recommend that you print it out and carry it with you as a reference once you're in Japan.

The Japan FAQ Know Before You Go Website
thejapanfaq.cjb.net
This one is a gold mine of information, however it is based on a British perspective, so some of the information may differ for American travelers. Nonetheless, the basic information is right on the mark.

Teaching English in Japan
www.wizweb.com/~susan/japan
A very thorough, firsthand perspective on the whole Japan experience.

Web sites for Employment
Ohayo Sensei
www.ohayosensei.com
By far the best and most abundant source for finding teaching opportunities in Japan. This site contains an impressive list of ads for English teachers in Japan, and also features a book list with over 1800 titles on Japanese culture, language, history, travel, and personal narratives. You can download the current issue online, or for a modest fee of $12 annually, the latest issue of Ohayo Sensei will be sent automatically to your e-mail address twice a month.

TEFL.com
www.tefl.com
This website features an extensive list of teaching opportunities worldwide. And although it does not focus exclusively on Japan, it regularly posts a promising list of Japanese help wanted ads. You can also subscribe to the Job Link bulletin and have new job postings sent to you by e-mail on a daily or weekly basis. In addition, this site has supplemental information on getting a TEFL certificate.

Jobs in Japan
www.jobsinjapan.com/
Another good source for seeking employment online. A substantial list of current job opportunities and links to other job resources as well.

Career Cross Japan
www.careercross.com
This site features a searchable database with which you can specify your preferred location, your level of experience and other criteria to find a perfect match. Be advised however, that much of Career Cross Japan's content is for jobs other than teaching. Therefore, their list of jobs for teachers may be less abundant than others.

Gaijin Pot
www.gaijinpot.com

A straightforward resource devoted exclusively to working in Japan. In addition to a long list of currently available jobs, the site contains links to other helpful resources and offers an option to have new job listings sent to you by e-mail

Interac
www.interac.co.jp/recruit

Interac specializes in recruiting English teachers for schools and corporations throughout Japan. Their website is a good starting place for getting advance job placement in Japan. If you meet the criteria, you may be able to proceed directly to "Go."

The Jet Program
www.mofa.go.jp/j_info/visit/jet/index.html

The Japan Exchange and Teaching Program (JET) is a government-sponsored program designed for Japanese junior and senior high school students to improve their spoken English language skills through exposure to native English speakers.

The JET program hires native speakers of English for the position of ALT (Assistant Language Teacher). If hired as an ALT, you may be placed in the city office where you will be sent out to schools to provide one-time lessons to help motivate students, or you may be assigned to specific schools for regular daily lessons. However, in this capacity, a JET teacher is always under the supervision of the regular classroom teacher, who will determine your role in the teaching process.

As an ALT for the JET program, at ¥300,000 per month, you can earn slightly more than the minimum offered at most private schools. The program also offers round-trip airline tickets and housing assistance.

You can apply for the JET program at a Japanese embassy or consulate, where you will also be interviewed. These positions are limited and highly competitive. The hiring process happens only once a year, beginning in December, with positions to commence the following Spring. The criteria specifies that applicants be college graduates under 35 years of age, and must not have resided in Japan for more than three of the past 10 years.

Complete details are available at the JET web site: **www.mofa.go.jp/j_info/visit/jet/index.html** You can also contact the JET offices at 1-800-INFO-JET (1-800-463-6538), or by postal mail at: JET Program, Embassy of Japan, 2520 Massachusetts Avenue, N.W., Washington, DC 20008.

Web sites for Temporary Lodging
International Tourist Center of Japan
www.itcj.or.jp/
This site is maintained by the International Tourist Center of Japan, and features an impressive list of lodgings in all price ranges and all regions of Japan.

Japan Youth Hostels, Inc.
www.jyh.or.jp/
This website is dedicated exclusively to youth hostels in Japan. It is well organized by region and city, and features hundreds of low cost lodging options.

Web sites for Apartments
Although the Internet is infinitely useful for all other elements of going to Japan to teach English, for several reasons, it is not nearly as useful for finding economical living quarters. While there are a limited number of web sites that offer apartments for rent, they are generally on the upper end of the price range, their availability is not always easy to determine, and of course, it is ill-advised to rent an apartment sight unseen, especially before you know for sure where you'll be working. However, with a keyword search using "apartments Japan" or "apartment rental" and the name of a specific city, you can get an idea of what's out there, and what your yen will buy in the rental real estate market. Some sites even include sample contracts and rental guidelines. So by all means, spend a little time browsing and familiarizing yourself with the rental game in Japan,

but don't expect to be able to find anything definitive online. When it comes to renting an apartment, you simply have to do it in person. And who knows, your employment package may include an apartment and thus allow you to skip this step altogether.

Using a Computer in Japan

If you are using this book in the way it was intended, while logged on to the Internet as you read, then chances are your computer is an integral and essential part of your lifestyle, and its absence would be sorely missed. Which begs the question: Will I be able to take my computer to Japan with me, or perhaps buy one while I'm there? Alas, this is a question more easily asked than answered.

Several factors must be considered when it comes to using your computer, or any computer for that matter, in Japan: cost and risk of shipping from home versus of cost to purchase in Japan, disparity of electrical current between the U.S. and Japan, modem compatibility, and cost of Internet connection.

Shipping your computer from home

By all accounts, this is not a good idea for several reasons. First of all, even by the most economical surface mail, to ship your CPU, monitor, keyboard, mouse, printer and all the other essential paraphernalia would cost over $100, and there's no guarantee that it would arrive intact. Of course you could insure it, but when all is said and done, you'd still be without a computer. Second, the electrical system in Japan does not function at the same frequency as electricity in the U.S., so you may not have enough power to operate it. And third, your modem may not be compatible with Japanese ISP servers. The consensus is that a laptop or notebook computer is your best bet. You can carry it on the plane with you, so there's no shipping, and charging the battery separately may be safer than plugging your system directly into an electrical outlet.

Purchasing a computer in Japan

The price of a new personal computer system in Japan is remarkably comparable to prices in the U.S. For as little as ¥100,000, which is about $800, you can purchase a basic desktop computer system. As in the U.S., you can spend a lot more if you wish, and peripherals such as a printer and scanner must be purchased separately. And of course software is another can of worms altogether. At the very least you will have to buy an English operating system such as Windows. But if you have a couple thousand extra dollars to spend on a computer, then spend and enjoy.

Alternatives

Although the process of setting yourself up with a computer system in Japan may be complex, it's not impossible. Even if you don't have an unlimited budget, there are still several economical alternatives that may work for you.

Buy Used

Here's where *sayonara* sales can really come to the rescue. With a little diligence, you can probably find a computer system for sale by an ex-pat who is packing it in and heading for home. Chances are, the price will be just right, and it will already be set up with all the peripherals and software you need.

Choose Kansai

If the electrical system is the only thing keeping you from bringing a computer to Japan, then look for work in the Kansai area, which includes the lovely cities of Kyoto, Osaka, Nagoya and Hiroshima. At 100 volts and 60 hz, the power system in Kansai is closer in strength to that of the U.S. than the weaker 100 volts and 50 hz of the Kanto area, which includes the cities of Tokyo and Yokohama. Either way, most computers will probably work okay, they'll just be a little slow.

Get a Japanese Modem

If you bring a computer to Japan and find that your modem doesn't function properly with Japanese ISP servers, you can always purchase a Japanese modem and install it in your computer. While Japanese modems may be more expensive than their American counterparts, this workaround is a viable alternative to an otherwise functional system.

Use an Information Service Center

Throughout Japan's major metropolitan areas, there are dozens of information service centers that specialize in serving the needs of business people on the go. In addition to their telephone messaging services, their business card and resume production services, and their conference rooms for rent by the hour, many information service centers offer Internet connection for a modest hourly fee. Granted you won't be able to spend hours surfing the 'Net, but you can send and receive e-mail and place orders for goods online. It's a convenient and economical alternative to bringing your own computer from home.

Take only your hard drive with you

This is a clever option for all you techno-savvy readers. Since all your data is stored on a hard drive that's no bigger than the average paperback book, you can remove it from your home system and carry it with you to Japan. Once you're settled, you can purchase a new or used Japanese computer system, install your own hard drive in it, and away you go. But be sure to research hardware compatibility in advance.

Information online

The JET Alumni Association has an excellent article containing detailed information on and suggestions for using a computer in Japan. You can read it in its entirety at
www.jetaasc.org/php/article.php?content=computers

The Internet in Japan

When it comes to Internet Service Providers and Internet fees, Japan is roughly on a par with the U.S. There are a number of ISP's to choose from, and at around ¥2000 per month, the rates in Japan are comparable to those in the U.S. But where the two systems diverge is in the toll fees for the use of the telephone line, which is charged at the local rate of about ¥10 per minute. That's equal to almost $5.00 per hour.

There are a couple of marginal alternatives, including a free temporary connection through an ISP called Live Door **www.livedoor.com** that offers dial-up access from most major cities in Japan. Sound too good to be true? Well it probably is. Unless you're fluent in Japanese, or have a native speaker to help you, chances are, you won't be able to figure out how to sign up for it because the entire site is in Japanese.

And for ¥1800 per month, NTT offers a service called Telehodai, which allows calls to two local numbers between the hours of 11 p.m. and 8 a.m. at no per-minute toll charge. Which is great if you can stay up all night and don't have to get up in the morning.

When it comes to Cable access and DSL, much of Japan is still behind the times, although Tokyo is a little better equipped than the rest of the country. At ¥6000 per month, the cost is similar to DSL, but availability is limited.

ISP Resources online

Internet.com offers a comprehensively cross-referenced compendium of Internet resources including Internet service providers world wide. The page containing links for Japan can be accessed at
http://thelist.internet.com/countrycode/81/

Notes:

Arriving in Japan

In the best of all possible worlds, when you arrive in Japan, you'll be met at the airport by several really cool English-speaking people in a mini-van, who will help you with your luggage and offer you a large, comfortable, conveniently located, rent-free, open-ended place to stay...Dream on, *tomodachi*.

Not to worry, though. Once you've awakened from your dream, the reality of getting settled in Japan isn't terribly difficult, provided you've done your homework. The most important element is finding lodging for the first few days. Your first impression of Japan will set the tone for your entire stay, so it's important to start off on the right foot with every available advantage.

It should also be mentioned here that the "best of all possible worlds" scenario does happen from time to time and should not be ruled out as a possibility. Always consider every option when beginning your search. Start at the top, and maximize all your resources. In the words of motivational speaker Les Brown, "Shoot for the moon. Even if you miss it you will land among the stars." Or in this case, in Japan.

First Impressions

No doubt, in the course of all your research you have seen hundreds of dazzlingly beautiful photographs of Japan. However, based on those images, you may be shocked and disappointed at your first impression of Japan on the trip into the city from the airport. With its futuristic design and peninsular location, Kansai International Airport may provide a pleasant welcome; but depending upon the time of day and the season in which you arrive, the skies are likely to be gray and the landscape barren in the area surrounding Narita. Moreover, transit trains do not provide the best venue for enjoying Japan's beauty, as the utilitarian architecture and other structures that are necessary elements of the railway system are rarely appealing to the eye. While this is not always the case, Japan's beauty is more often discovered through the windows of cross-country trains, and in unexpected, up-close vignettes while traveling on foot.

On Your Own

Those who do not already have permanent lodging arrangements through friends or an employer will probably have to rough it for a few days or weeks in a family-style *ryokan*, a youth hostel, a *gaijin* house with rooms for rent, or, if you're lucky, on a futon in someone's spare *tatami* room. Here's where all your stateside research pays off. If you can find even one friend-of-a-friend to put you up for a few days, consider yourself among the truly blessed. And, in the event that you *are* that lucky, be sure to practice good houseguest etiquette: Shoes off at the front door, respectful use of kitchen and bath, observance of household waking and bedtime schedules, clean up after yourself, keep your belongings out of the way, offer to buy groceries and household supplies, and of course, present your hosts with thoughtful hospitality gifts when you arrive. See Chapter Ten for gift suggestions.

Key Criteria to Consider When Choosing Your First Lodgings

Price

Budget lodging in Japan can cost anywhere from ¥2000 to ¥10,000 per night. In U.S. dollars, that's a range of $16-$80. At the low end of the spectrum, amenities are likely to include little more than a futon on the floor of a six *tatami* room and a shared bathroom. In the mid-range, a Japanese-style breakfast of rice, miso soup and salted fish, may be included. And for a premium price, you might find a room with a western-style bed and bath, with both breakfast and dinner included. With the objective of making your money last as long as possible, it's wise to go for less expensive lodgings. But be sure to inquire about the condition of the rooms and bathrooms, and which amenities are included. In Japan, you will find that even the most rustic establishments are clean and safe, and the proprietors are friendly and gracious. However, it's best to research several establishments from home and bring the information with you for a handy list of alternatives to fall back on in the event that the place you've chosen is unacceptable when you arrive. And even if you like the lodgings, it's probably best to pay as you go, as refunds are unlikely. This will allow you to remain flexible in case you find something better, or you get hired and find a place to live right away.

Proximity to the Train or Subway Station

You'll be on foot for much of the first few days, so every step counts. Try to choose centrally located lodgings if possible and affordable. Room rates are lower in the suburbs, but the train rides take longer to get to the inner city. If you do end up staying outside the city, the transit system in Japan is still very efficient and easily accessible, even from the outer suburbs. This is where a map comes in handy. As you research jobs and lodgings, mark them on the map and make your choices accordingly. One key point to remember is that although the distance from place to place may not appear to be very far, the train has to stop at every little station along the way. So a distance of only a few miles can take up to an hour to reach. On certain transit lines however, there are express trains that only stop at major hubs. They travel at greater speeds, but also have their own specific schedules and run less frequently than the local trains that stop at every station.

It is also possible to purchase a monthly rail pass that allows unlimited daily travel on a particular transit line. However, rail passes are priced according to the number of train stations they encompass, and any destination beyond the stations included in your pass, or those located on another transit line, have to be paid for separately. So, if the job opportunities you discover in your research are all within a concentrated area in which you can also find lodging, a rail pass that includes all those locations may be an economical way to travel while you're looking for work and a permanent home. And of course, a rail pass is essential once you've found work and a place to live. In fact, many employers include a monthly rail pass in their employment benefits package.

Telephone Access for Making and Receiving Calls

This is a must. Most ads list a telephone number to call for setting up an interview. Calling from a pay phone can be awkward and noisy, so a private phone in a quiet setting would be ideal. And of course, being able to receive calls from prospective employers or landlords is an obvious necessity. You may even wish to investigate wireless telephone access. Cell phones are ubiquitous in Japan. However, the difficult obstacle to overcome in setting up wireless service in Japan before you've gotten settled will be the lack of a bank account and a permanent address for billing. However, there are even several international wireless service providers whose phones and calling plans may be purchased before you travel. They can be considerably more expensive than domestic calling plans, but for the savvy job seeker, this would be an especially valuable asset. A third option is to utilize the services of a commercial information center such as the Kimi Center **www2.dango.ne.jp/kimi/index.html** near the west exit of Ikebukero Station in Tokyo. For a modest fee, they will receive your telephone calls and take messages for you. They also produce resumes and business cards, and provide access to fax machines, computers, internet connections, and meeting rooms.

Your First Day in Japan

Let's assume you've gotten yourself to Japan, traded some of your domestic money for ¥50,000 or so at the airport currency exchange, successfully navigated your way to your first night's lodgings, and opened your eyes the following morning (or evening) wondering just what planet you've woken up on...Don't panic. More importantly, unless you have a host or friend to show you around, don't try to accomplish anything more ambitious on your first day than taking a walk around the neighborhood, maybe having a bowl of noodles, getting your hands on a public transit map, buying yourself a copy of the *Japan Times*, the *Asahi Shimbun* and the *Yomuri Daily*. These English versions of three popular Japanese newspapers may be purchased almost exclusively at kiosks inside the train stations, or in the sundries shops of large hotels. You might stumble upon the occasional newsstand out in the suburbs, but it's not likely. Look for newspapers inside the nearest train station.

Once you've accomplished these humble tasks and found your way back to your lodgings, have some green tea, browse through your newspapers, take a hot bath, go back to bed, and sleep off the jetlag. After all, in the immortal words of Scarlett O'Hara (who most certainly never faced the stygian task of apartment and job hunting in Japan), "Tomorrow is another day."

Jet Lag

According to some authorities on the subject, to recover from jet lag, it takes one day for each time zone you cross. Of course this phenomenon varies from one person to the next, but you can expect to feel a little out of sorts for a week or so until you reestablish your circadian rhythms. In addition to disturbances in sleep patterns, intercontinental travel can cause dehydration and fatigue. However, there are steps you can take to significantly minimize the effects of extended air travel. The first and most important piece of advice is to drink lots of water, not only while you're in the air, but also during the days before your flight. Another effective tip is to set your watch to the local time of your destination as soon as you get on the plane, and act accordingly. Throughout your trip, eat your meals and try to get as much sleep as possible in sync with the corresponding times in Japan. Avoid alcohol and salty foods, and to help you sleep, use earplugs and a sleep mask if necessary. Get up occasionally to stretch and move about, wear comfortable, loose-fitting clothes and shoes, or bring some to change into once you're on the plane. Holistic practitioner, Dr. Andrew Weil, M.D., has an excellent online Q&A forum on his website Ask Dr. Weil. **www.askdrweil.com** Using the keywords "jet lag" you can find more tips and suggestions to help you feel your best once you've arrived in Japan.

The Coin of the Realm

Japanese yen are minted in six different values of coins and three different denominations of paper. Change is circulated as ¥1, ¥5, ¥10 , ¥50, ¥100, and ¥500 coins. Paper currency is circulated as ¥1000, ¥5000, and ¥10,000 bills.

¥1 coins are made of aluminum, and are so light and lacking in substance that the slightest breeze will blow them right out of your hand. Perhaps the lightweight composition of these lowliest of Japanese coins is an obvious metaphor for what it will buy in Japan: absolutely nothing. In the contemporary economy, single yen coins are used mainly to make change for the uneven purchase amounts created by the addition of the 5% consumption tax levied on nearly every transaction in Japan. Don't be surprised to find these ethereal coins scattered about on the city sidewalks, because once they're dropped, nobody even bothers to bend and pick them up.

¥5 coins have the classic Asian brass design with a hole in the center. Interestingly, the ¥5 coin is the only piece of Japanese currency that has no Western numbers or letters on it. Although they don't buy much, they're quite beautiful.

¥10 coins are bulky copper pieces used frequently in everyday circulation as Japan's conventional pricing structure favors ¥90 endings. Much like 99¢ in the U.S., where many items are priced at $1.99, $3.99, $29.99, etc., in Japan, it's ¥290, ¥490, ¥1590, etc.

¥50 coins are made of a silver/nickel alloy and also have a hole in the middle. Depending upon the currency exchange rate, they are nearly equivalent to an American half dollar, yet they spend like an American quarter.

At ¥100, Japanese coins begins to take on some substance. The lower denominations are mere pocket change, but a ¥100 coin will actually buy something, albeit not much more than a pack of gum or a small beverage. But for that same reason, a few ¥100 pieces in your coin purse can add up to the equivalent of a $10 bill, and can also slip through your fingers before you know it. So don't be fooled…Treat them like dollar bills.

¥500 pieces are an interesting concept for Westerners, who tend to think of coins as insignificant pocket change. But these coins actually amount to almost five dollars apiece, and with only a few of them in your pocket or coin purse, you could easily find yourself toting the equivalent of $20 or $30 in change. So here's a word of caution for those on a tight budget, or anyone trying to put a little money aside: Watch how you spend your change. It's not uncommon to get to the end of the day and wonder where your money went, only to add it up and find that you dribbled it away ¥500 at a time on train tickets, chewing gum, newspapers, soda, and other sundries.

¥1000 bills have a picture of Natsume Soseki, Japan's most beloved author on them. They are valued somewhere between a U.S. $5 and $10 bill, and much like the ¥500 coin, it's easy to let them slip through your fingers. They add up, so watch how you spend them.

A Japanese ¥5000 bill spends about like an American $20 (if you're thrifty, perhaps a bit more). But expect to average going through one of these on a typical outing, whether it's a casual day trip, or a modest night on the town.

¥10,000 bills are the C-notes of Japan, but carry far less prestige. They are ubiquitous in everyday spending, and are only equal to about $80, which will vanish faster than you can say, "I'll have the blowfish."

As for carrying all that money around, it's *de rigueur* in Japan. Everybody uses cash as the preferred method of payment for almost all transactions. The "checking account" system is unheard of, and credit cards haven't quite caught on yet as an alternative to plain old cash. And with the remarkably low incidence of violent crime in Japan, there's no need to worry about carrying a modest amount of it around with you on an everyday basis. The biggest drawback to this is the temptation to spend it.

Notes:

Landing a Job in Japan

These are the three crucial elements you will need to land a job teaching English in Japan: A university degree, adequate documentation and a proactive approach, all of which should be completed, prepared and implemented before you leave home. There are also a number of surefire strategies for a successful interview. While some of them are unique to the Japanese culture, with few exceptions, they are based primarily on common sense and common courtesy.

Three Crucial Elements

A University Degree and a Teaching Certificate

The best asset for finding a job teaching English in Japan is a BA or better in English, a TEFL Certification, or both. And although a teaching certificate is not essential, and it is possible to find work with a college degree in a subject other than English, your earning potential is greatly enhanced with an educational background in the English language.

In your research, you may encounter the terms TEFL and TESL and wonder what is the difference. TEFL (Teaching English as a Foreign Language) is essentially a British term and TESL (Teaching English as a Second Language) is an American term. The distinction is made between teaching English to non-native speakers in a non-English speaking country (EFL) and teaching English to non-native speakers in an English-speaking country (ESL). However, these terms seem to be interchangeable among teachers abroad.

There are dozens of universities and commercial schools that offer TEFL and TESL programs. The certification generally requires 120 hours of classroom time over the course of four weeks for full time, or twelve weeks for part time study. Tuition for the program ranges from approximately $750 to $2500, depending upon each individual institution. A university degree may or may not be a pre-requisite for enrollment. To enroll in a TEFL or TESL program, inquire at your local university, or visit TEFL.com **www.tefl.com** for a list of schools.

You can also earn a TEFL certificate online in a two-week intensive training course through The TEFL Center **www.teflcenter.com** for a tuition fee of $399. The Open Learning International **www.olionline.com** is another website that offers the OCR (Oxford, Cambridge RSA) Certificate in Teaching Foreign Languages to Adults The full course is available via the Internet and can be completed at your own pace for a tuition fee ranging from $900 to $1500.

Adequate Documentation

When packing your belongings to take to Japan, be sure to include the following documents to give to prospective employers: a dozen or so copies of your diploma, your teaching certificate, your college transcripts, any awards or honors you've won, your birth certificate, any letters of recommendation you may have, a well-composed and polished resume, and an abundant stash of tasteful, passport-quality photos of yourself. In some case, you may be asked to provide a photo, especially for official government applications. Note however, that only originals of your diploma and university transcripts and birth certificate are acceptable for a work visa application, so be sure to bring them along with you. The copies are just for your job interview presentation.

Another good rule of thumb is to include a photo of yourself with every resume you submit. In fact, if you have access to a computer and a scanner, you can copy and paste your photo directly into your resume and print out several dozen copies to take with you to Japan. A professional-looking photo of yourself will make you appear especially job-worthy and will help keep you fresh and foremost in the minds of potential employers. Refer to Chapter Twelve for tips on composing a sharp resume.

A Proactive Approach

Veterans of the quest for English teaching positions in Japan strongly advise that you apply in person only. While this is essentially sound advice, another very effective approach is to target your prospects via the Internet and send your resume a few weeks ahead of time to any schools or companies that appear viable. Let them know when you'll be arriving in Japan, and parlay that initial contact into an appointment for an interview. This tiny bit of effort may help you avoid pounding the pavement altogether. It certainly worked for me.

Tips for a Winning Interview

Know Your Prospective Employer

Find out anything you can about the company ahead of time. Ask questions on the phone when making an appointment for an interview. If you have a computer and the company has a website, research it on the Internet. Ask the locals if they are familiar with the school or company. Observe the quality of neighborhood and the building when you arrive. Take notice of its promotional literature, or lack of it. Discreetly talk to people who are already employed there if possible. If it appears disreputable or strange in any way, keep your radar sharp and be ready to bow out if you can't picture yourself working there.

Be Punctual

Japan is a society that demands, nay thrives upon punctuality, so no matter how early you have to get up, or how lost you might get along the way, arrive on time. The train system runs like clockwork, and melodic chimes can be heard marking the hour in almost every public building. Tardiness is frowned upon, so by all means, make sure you get detailed directions, research your route beforehand and give yourself adequate time for a punctual arrival for your interview.

Make a Good First Impression

As you'll soon discover, Japan is a conservative culture when it comes to business (and most everything else, too.) And although the teaching environment at some establishments can be somewhat casual, it's important to make a good first impression. So wear tasteful clothing to your interviews (a suit and tie for the gents;

a skirt, blouse and jacket for the ladies). Jewelry and accessories should be modest, hair should be neatly styled, shoes should be comfortable, practical and freshly polished, and beware of holes in your socks or stockings. You never know when you may be expected to remove your shoes.

Pay Close Attention to the Place and the People

When you arrive at your interview, take a moment to intuit the atmosphere. Is it upscale and Westernized, befitting a firm handshake? Or does it appear traditional, where bowing and leaving your shoes at the door would be more appropriate? Use your best judgment in that initial encounter.

And never underestimate the power of a well-timed hajime-mashite (nice to meet you) or a domo arigato (thank you very much) to make a good impression. Even if you only know a few words of Japanese, make good use of them for a winning first impression.

Observe the hierarchy of rank: Who's the boss? Who's asking the questions? And wait until you're invited before being seated. If business cards are exchanged, treat any you receive with the utmost reverence. Admire it, nod politely and place it respectfully into your valise, not in your pocket or your wallet. Otherwise, hang on to it discreetly, and whatever you do, don't leave it behind on the desk or the table when the interview is over.

Be Confident yet Conservative

By nature, the Japanese people are modest and unassuming. They are reluctant to accept compliments, and rarely boast about their talents and accomplishments. Self-aggrandizement is considered rude and boorish. Consequently, a job applicant attempting to adhere to this convention faces the dilemma of trying to appear highly qualified for the job without acting like the Cock of the Walk. Under these circumstances, discretion and moderation are key: Bow, but not too deeply; smile, but not too broadly; laugh, but not too effusively; joke, but not too presumptuously; list your qualifications, but don't brag; and most important of all, listen carefully and ask intelligent questions.

Arrive Organized & Well Prepared

Have all your paperwork at hand in a lightweight, stylish valise or portfolio, including resumes, photos, diplomas, transcripts, certificates, awards, and anything else that might enhance your chances of being hired. These documents should be neatly assembled for presentation during the interview so that you don't have to shuffle through everything in your valise to find your papers. And even if you were a straight-A student and graduated with honors, you'd be wise to brush up on your English terminology. It's easy to forget if you haven't used it for a while. Make sure you know your *modal auxiliaries* from your *plu perfects*. You may even be expected to give a brief sample lesson, so prepare one in advance, just in case you're asked to do so. See Chapter Nine for sample lesson ideas.

Watch Your Language

During the interview, sit up straight, speak clearly and confidently, use good diction and grammar, and never, ever use profanity of any kind. Remember, you're being interviewed for the purpose of teaching others how to speak. Rest assured, they'll be hanging on your every word.

Be Prepared to Make a Decision

Not every interview concludes with a firm job offer, but many do. If they like you, they may just offer you a contract on the spot. So listen carefully to the requirements and benefits of the job throughout the interview. Ask all relevant questions when given the opportunity. And remember, out there on the pavement, the competition is stiff, it's a monster of a city, and it's expensive. Few, if any jobs in Japan are perfect, but if one comes even close, go for it and give it your best effort. If nothing else, it will give you a foothold from which to seek greener pastures. Be advised however, that job-hopping is frowned upon by Japanese employers and should be kept to a minimum. And while it is perfectly understandable for a newcomer to strike out on the first try, a string of short-lived jobs should be avoided if possible. If not, it should be downplayed on your resume for future interviews.

Wherever You Go, There You Are

The world of business in Japan differs from the politically correct strictures of the U.S. in that Japanese employers may unabashedly specify a preferred gender, age or nationality in their classified ads; and getting a work visa requires the sponsorship of a Japanese citizen. However, with the exception of these and a few other cultural idiosyncrasies, job seeking in Japan is much the same as anywhere else. It's ubiquitous and it's competitive. Therefore, just as one would embark on a quest for employment at home, the surest way to succeed in Japan is to research the market, get yourself organized, look sharp, and convince them that you're the one they want for the job.

Notes:

Finding a Place to Live

The most important thing to remember in your search for a place to call your own in Japan is that the rules as you know them no longer apply. Any notions you may have about apartment size, price, amenities, rent control, fair housing, etc., should be left at the door with your shoes. Japan is a culture unto itself, and therefore it's best not to compare it with the familiar conventions and commodities of home. Almost every element of life in Japan will be different from life as you know it. And although it is possible to live quite comfortably in Japan, it still takes a lot of getting used to. But countless thousands of people have done it and are doing it every day. So can you.

What's a 2LDK?

Apartments in Japan are measured in *tatami*, a unit based on woven rice straw floor mats approximately one meter wide by two meters long. Many Japanese apartments actually have *tatami* floors, but even if they don't, they're still measured in *tatami*. And the realtors' shorthand for the features of a dwelling is abbreviated to the number of bedrooms and the initials for living room, dining room and kitchen. So a 2LDK is an apartment with two bedrooms, a living room, dining room and kitchen. Sometimes these are individual rooms, and sometimes they are combined. Other listed features might include a private bathroom, a western-style toilet, a *furo* bathtub, a small garden, a balcony, or some household furnishings.

Apartments are also categorized and valued by their location on a certain transit line and their proximity to the nearest train station. And some apartments called *mansions* are really just modern apartment buildings, not grand estates as the name might imply, although some can be quite expensive and come with all the finest amenities. On the other end of the spectrum, many apartments are quite small and rustic, with no air conditioning, little heat, and offer only communal toilets with no bathing facilities. Tenants of such places must rely on the public *sento* baths for their daily hygiene. So, as you can see, the range of living alternatives is quite diverse.

Addresses in Japan

Unlike the U.S., in Japan, not every street has a name, and even the streets that do have names often have no street signs to identify them. Instead, cities are divided into a series of graduated units. First, there's the *ken*, or prefecture, which is a large regional unit. Each *ken* is divided into wards called *ku*. And each *ku* contains a number of small cities or suburbs, which are further divided into districts or neighborhoods called *chome*. The *chome* are divided into smaller grids called *ban*, and individual buildings are called *go*, all three of which are identified only by numbers. Finally comes the building name, if it has one, and the apartment number. Japan also uses a zip code system. My address in Japan, (a building that, alas, is no longer standing) was #101 Ikebukuro Flat, 3-17-18 Nishi Ikebukuro, Toshima-ku, Tokyo, 171. So I lived in the zip code #171, in Tokyo *ken*, Toshima *ku*, on the *nishi* (west) side of the city suburb of Ikebukuro, in the third *chome*, in *ban* 17, *go* 18, in a building named Ikebukuro Flat, Apartment #101. However, when the Japanese address an envelope, they write all that information in reverse, beginning with the *ken*, *ku*, and zip. But your mail will find you either way.

As for navigating your way about in Japan, the convention for giving directions to specific locations in large metropolitan areas tends to be more visual than verbal. Tiny maps are often printed on advertisements and on the backs of business cards; and when someone gives you directions, they are more likely to draw you a map than to name off the streets and turns you would take to get there. And when looking at apartments, the landlord will probably offer to meet you at the train station and guide you there in person. If you decide to rent the apartment, be sure to take notes on your way back to the station so you can find your way there again by yourself.

How Does One Go About Finding an Apartment in Japan?

The task of finding permanent lodgings in Japan can be time-consuming, confusing and expensive. Therefore it is important to keep your research materials organized, take detailed notes on prospective apartments, and if at all possible, ask a Japanese person to help you in your search. The following information and suggestions will facilitate the process.

Look everywhere. Look in the newspapers. Ask around the neighborhood. If you've already been hired, ask around the school or office. Talk to people, both foreign and domestic. Search online if you have Internet access. And keep your eyes peeled for rental agencies. You'll come to recognize them by the dozens of apartment listings posted in the shop windows detailing the number of *tatami*, the monthly rent, the deposit expected, any furnishings or amenities, the nearest train station, etc. They really are quite informative, and you may just find your dream home. The one we lucked into was eighteen *tatami*, ten minutes' walk from the train station, with a tiny garden, a western toilet, five rooms, fully furnished right down to the chopsticks, a gas heater, a washer, a sewing machine, and…a piano! All for only ¥90,000 and two hours of our time on our days off, teaching English to the landlady's daughters, and a group of darling Japanese children in her little English cram school in Toshimaen. So, have faith! There are bargains to be had.

Be punctual, sincere, and well prepared. Once you schedule an appointment with a rental agent or a landlord, be sure to arrive at exactly the appointed hour. Realtors and landlords don't typically live on the premises and therefore don't like to be kept waiting around for you to show up. When you meet, be extremely polite, bow deeply, greet them in Japanese if you know how, have all your paperwork at hand (passport, letters of recommendation or guarantorship, employment verification if you have it, bank account identification, etc.) and an attractive envelope with exactly the prescribed deposit money all ready to hand over at the appointed moment. The more information and validation you can provide, the more likely you are to walk away with the keys to the place.

Three Main Points to Remember When Deciding on an Apartment

Pay close attention to the neighborhood, the apartment, and the terms of the rental agreement.
On your way to view an apartment, observe carefully the route to it from the train station. If it's the one you choose to rent, it will become your local habitat and a significant part of your daily commute. Is it close to the train station and shopping? How far is it from your job? Is the neighborhood clean and quiet? Is there an after-hours convenience store? Is there a park nearby? Are the neighbors friendly? These elements will contribute greatly to the quality of everyday life while you're in Japan.

And when discussing the property with the agent or landlord, be sure to ask all pertinent questions about the terms of the lease. Is non-refundable "key money" expected? Are utilities included? Will you be allowed to make any changes in the décor? Are there any hidden costs? Is there any kind of stipulation, such as "No Visitors," a shared bathroom, or an obligation to teach private English lessons to the proprietor's children? Is there any chance that the apartment will be taken over unexpectedly by a relative in need? When faced with such caveats, give adequate consideration to your ability to tolerate and adhere to the conditions before committing to the rental agreement.

Take your time when looking at an apartment. Examine each room thoroughly, along with the exterior of the building. Be sure to note any pre-existing damages such as scratches, dents, tears or stains. And make sure that you fully understand the terms of the lease. What is the duration of the contract? What happens if you move out before the completion of the lease? What happens if you want to stay longer? What conditions might result in the forfeiture of your deposit? What are the terms for arbitration in the event of a dispute?

If at all possible, it would be wise to ask a Japanese friend or co-worker to accompany you to help bridge the language gap and avoid any potential misunderstandings. Don't be afraid to ask someone to act as a liaison.

Choose carefully.

It can be both difficult and costly to extricate yourself from a rental agreement in Japan. At best, you may have to forfeit a sizeable deposit. At worst, you could end up in court. While some conflicts cannot be foreseen, many can be avoided by being realistic and using common sense when it comes to signing a rental agreement. Only agree to terms that you're certain you can honor.

But Don't Be too Picky.

One definitely has to lower the bar when searching for an apartment in Japan. The Japanese affectionately refer to urban housing as *usagi no uchi*...rabbit warrens! With that in mind, be advised that some of the best bargains to be found are six-*tatami* rooms in aging wooden buildings with no kitchen, a squat toilet and a shared bath. Many of them are a hefty hike from the nearest train station, and no matter how small, quaint, inconveniently located, and lacking in amenities, *all* are overpriced.

On the positive side however, there is a certain charm and simplicity to the traditional Japanese way of life. It's clean, functional and uncluttered. And within that lifestyle, it's easy to make maximum use of minimum space. So don't be afraid to fully immerse yourself in the Japanese way of life. The thing to keep in mind is that, once you're earning yen as an English teacher, it's all relative, and quite easy to live within your means. Ultimately, the secret is to find the best place you can afford on your salary, and make the best of it.

Getting Hooked

Some apartments in Japan include utilities, while others do not. In the event that the one you rent falls into the latter category, your real estate agent or your landlord may be willing to help you with the process. Otherwise, here's how to go about getting your utilities hooked up.

For the electricity, look around for the circuit breaker. Once you locate it, you should find a post card with the name of the former tenant and the last meter reading. This post card can also be used as your application for your electric account. Once you fill it out, you can mail it in or take it to the electric company in person, which may be more expeditious. For water and gas, you will have to call or go to the water and gas departments at your local ward office to set up an account.

The process of getting a telephone is considerably more costly, and a little different from U.S conventions. For a private telephone line, you will first need a subscription permit, which you can buy from NTT, or from a broker, or even another individual, who may sell you theirs for less than the NTT rate. You may also obtain phone service from a private company, however it may not include international calls.

A subscription permit from NTT costs about ¥75,000, plus additional installation charges of ¥2,000, plus the 5% consumption tax. If you buy a phone line from another person, there is an added fee of ¥840.

The basic monthly fee for rotary phone service costs around ¥2,400. If you use a touch-tone phone, there is an extra monthly charge of ¥390, plus tax and a ¥2,000 installation fee. In addition to the monthly rate, each time you make a call, you will be charged a toll of ¥9 for each three minutes within your local ward, and ¥10 per 90 seconds to an adjacent ward. Long distance calls to other areas of Japan are charged at varying rates depending up on the distance and the time of day. You can also find discounted rates through private long distances companies such as Daini Denden, Japan Telecom and Nippon Kosoku Tsushin.

Feathering your nest

Once you have rented an apartment, unless it came fully furnished, you will need to fill it with furniture and everyday household amenities. As you may have already guessed, buying new furniture in Japan can be quite costly, not to mention the exorbitant fees for having it delivered to your home. However, Tokyo also has second-hand shops, which can be found in the Yellow Pages under the heading "Recycle." But again, there is the problem of getting your purchases home.

And as an economical alternative, there are two widely practiced methods of getting furnished: Sayonara sales, and scavenging.

Sayonara Sales

Since the cost of shipping goods out of Japan is quite expensive, most foreigners sell all their household belongings before they head home. Items such as furniture, bicycles, and even private telephone lines can be found in newspaper classifieds, on bulletin boards at the school where you work, and in places where foreigners hang out. But again, getting these bulky items home is another story. You may have to appeal to a neighbor with a vehicle, or a commercial delivery service.

Scavenging

Another unspoken yet widely practiced method of obtaining household furnishings is to keep an eye out on the streets in your immediate neighborhood on the nights before trash pick up. You will be amazed at the perfectly good household castoffs that people put out at the curb to be hauled away. So as long as you're not too proud to use someone else's discards, it's okay to help yourself to whatever you find on the street. Just be absolutely sure that it's actually being discarded, and don't help yourself to anything in broad daylight. Although it's perfectly legal, it's one of those things that is discreetly overlooked in polite society.

Smaller household items, such as wastebaskets, dishes, cookware, kitchen utensils and linens can be purchased at one of many neighborhood sundries shops. Similar to the 99¢ stores that have sprung up throughout the U.S., these shops carry a wide variety of inexpensive plasticware and discount items at modest prices. Chances are, there will be one of these shops in the neighborhood where you live or work.

Bringing electrical appliances from home

Bringing electrical appliances from home to Japan is like a game of roulette. Unlike the U.S., which operates at 120 volts, the Japanese electrical system operates on 100 volts. Further, the eastern Kanto area where Tokyo and Yokohama are located, uses 50Hz, while the western Kansai area where Osaka and Kyoto are located, uses 60Hz. Which means that a U.S. appliance that typically requires 60Hz may work fine when plugged into an outlet in Kyoto, but may run a little slowly or not at all in Yokohama. And even if there's enough juice to run your U.S. appliance, depending on the design of the plug, it may not fit into the Japanese electrical outlet. Bottom line: you're probably better off leaving your electrical gadgets at home, and either do without them in Japan, or budget for their purchase once you're earning a regular paycheck. Again, here is where sayonara sales and scavenging come into play.

Because of the electrical disparity between the U.S. and Japan, most foreigners jettison their belongings before they leave, so it's possible to find a good bargain on just the item you need from a departing teacher. And at the end of your stay, you can recoup some of your investment when you leave by having a sayonara sale of your own.

With regard to scavenging for electrical appliances, when they are put out to pasture, their owners generally snip off the plug, and sometimes the whole cord, thus rendering it useless to all except someone who feels confident enough to go to the local hardware store for a replacement cord to rewire it. Which isn't unheard of, but a risky endeavor nonetheless.

For purchasing new appliances, at least in Tokyo that is, the electronic shopping district of Akihabara is probably your best bet.

Notes:

Getting a Work Visa

If you think going to the DMV is a pain in the you-know-what, just wait 'til you've done time at the Immigration Office in downtown Tokyo. On my first visit there, I arrived just minutes after the lunch break ended, and already the place was packed with every imaginable form of humanity, all of them with eyes transfixed on the little red digital "Now Being Served" counter. I took a number, sat down in one of the few remaining seats, did the math and realized that there were two hundred and seventeen people in line ahead of me. I am not kidding. Two hundred and seventeen. And still people were pouring in, each one taking a number, doing the math, and rolling their eyes with a sigh of exasperation. Luckily I had brought along an anthology of *Calvin and Hobbes* cartoons, so I giggled and snickered my way through the whole affair. I heartily recommend you do the same.

But seriously, unless you have already been hired and have secured a work visa before you leave home, the process goes something like this:

You arrive in Japan with your passport and receive a 90-day landing permit (tourist visa). Or you can apply for it at the Japanese embassy or consulate from home before you leave for Japan if you wish. You may also have to show a return airline ticket with a departure date of no more than 90 days, to prove that you don't intend to overstay.

Next, you get yourself a job teaching English at a company that is willing to sponsor your work visa. It's a little like being bonded. Your sponsor is someone (preferably a Japanese businessman) who is willing to vouch for your character, integrity and good conduct while you're working in Japan. So unless you have made your own arrangements for a private sponsor, getting hired by a company that will sponsor your work visa is a crucial element. You can't get one without a sponsor.

Next, you'll have to apply for a Certificate of Eligibility (eligibility to obtain a work visa, that is). Your employer will provide you with the forms and help you fill out the paperwork. Once the forms have been submitted, you will receive your certificate by mail in 30 to 90 days.

But until you're officially documented with a work visa, you'll have to apply for an Alien Registration Card at your local ward office, which is similar to a county office in the U.S. You'll need an Alien Registration card to use as an I.D. to set up a bank account so you can receive your paycheck. Those companies that do not pay in cash typically transfer your monthly salary directly to your bank account instead of issuing a paycheck. And while we're on the subject, your employer will usually let you know which bank they prefer and ask you to set up an account there.

Back to the Alien Registration card: Until you receive your work visa, technically speaking, you're not supposed to work while you're still on a tourist visa, but since it's the one glitch that can't be avoided, most people do it anyway, with no negative consequences. Just be sure to carry your Alien Registration card with you at all times.

Once you receive your Certificate of Eligibility, it's time to apply for a work visa at a Japanese Embassy (outside Japan, of course). Many people fly to Seoul because it's the closest and least expensive. While you're there, you'll get your work visa stamped into your passport.

When you arrive at the Japanese Embassy to apply for a visa, you must present several documents: one provided by your employer describing the activities of the business, the duration of your contract, the position you've been hired for, and the salary you will be paid, this along with your original college diploma and transcripts, your TEFL certificate if you have one, and of course, your passport.

Once you've completed your application, it usually takes two to three days to process; and unless your job doesn't begin right away and you plan to do a bit of extended sightseeing, once you get your work visa stamped into your passport, it's off you go on the next flight back to Japan.

While You're in Seoul

As one might expect, the Japanese Embassy in Seoul is located right downtown. You should go here first thing to get your paperwork started, as the visa application may take a couple of days to process. No matter where you stay in Seoul, the subway system will take you there. Write the address of the Embassy on a piece of paper and show it to the stationmaster for directions to the train that will take you there.

The Japanese Embassy in Seoul is located at the following address:

Embassy of Japan

Kyobo Building , Ninth Floor
Chongro 1-ka, Chongro-ku,
Seoul, Republic of Korea
Tel:(82-2)733-5626, 739-7400
Fax:(82-2)734-4528, 739-7410

When to Go (or Rather, When Not to Go)

The Korean calendar is based on the lunar phases and therefore the exact dates of the holidays vary from one year to the next. There are two major holiday seasons in Korea: The Lunar New Year, which falls on the first day of the first moon, usually sometime in January; and the Harvest Moon Festival, a thanksgiving celebration held on the 15th day of the eighth month, which occurs sometime in late September or early October. On both occasions, the entire country takes a holiday. Travel accommodations are all booked up and businesses are closed. Therefore it's wise to check the exact dates of these celebrations and plan your trip accordingly.

The Korean Won

Over a two-year average, the Korean won has been trading at about 10 won to the Japanese yen and about 1200 won to the U.S. dollar.

While exchange rates can fluctuate dramatically, these rates can be used as a general index to help you calculate the cost of your trip to Seoul.

Korean Currency almost exactly mirrors that of Japan, with paper denominations in 10,000, 5,000 and 1,000 won; and coins in 500, 100, 50 and 10 won pieces.

Once you've finished your business in Seoul and you're ready to depart, those in the know recommend that you exchange your won back into yen before you leave Seoul because it's difficult and costly to do so once you're back in Japan.

Travel from the Airport to the City Center

Most major international airlines fly into South Korea's Kimp'o Airport, which is about 8 miles west of downtown Seoul. However, the trip can take up to an hour. The airport terminal is serviced by an extensive network of buses that run between the hours of 5:30 a.m. and midnight. Taxis and private airport shuttles also transport passengers from the airport to the city center, and Seoul has a public transit system that consists of eight subway lines to serve the metropolitan area. The subway system is quite efficient and provides very helpful maps in English.

Where to Stay

In the city of Seoul, accommodations run the gamut, from luxury hotels with all the amenities, to bare-bones, "Motel-6-ish" type establishments and traditional-style inns. The deluxe accommodations, priced between 200,000 to 300,000 won per night ($150-$250 U.S., or ¥20,000 to ¥30,000), are mostly in the area around the centrally located City Hall Square.

More modest accommodations, priced at 75,000 to 100,000 won per night ($60-$80 U.S., or ¥7500 to ¥10,000), can be found in the shopping and entertainment district of It'aewon, although it's a little out of the way and questionably safe at night.

Rock-bottom budget hotels come in the form of local establishments called *yogwan*, easily recognizable by the "steaming bowl" icons on their signs that supposedly represent "warmth. " *Yogwans* typically include a private bath and color TV, and at 25,000 won per night (about $20 U.S., or ¥2500), they're your best bargain when it comes to accommodations, as amenities vary little from place to place and the per-diem rate is fixed by law. *Yogwans* can be found in Kanghwamun, near the Sejong Cultural Center, and in the district of Insadong, on the south end of Seoul Station. So if you're feeling brave and want to save a few won/yen/bucks, don't bother making reservations beforehand, just go to one of these districts when you arrive and get yourself a room...as long as you remember not to travel when the locals are celebrating one of their moons.

Where and What to Eat

There's more to Korean food than the ubiquitous *kimchee*. The cuisine of Korea is a flavorful adventure, spiced with ginger, garlic, soy sauce, onions and chili peppers. Korean barbecue, known to the locals as *pulgoki*, is a hands-on experience in which the diners get to play chef at individual braziers recessed into each table. On a typical Korean menu, you will also find *kalbi*, charcoal grilled beef ribs; and meat-filled *mandu* dumplings, which can be ordered either steamed or fried. Not to worry, however. Less intrepid diners can play it safe with more familiar international dishes, such as pizza and hamburgers, which are readily available at a growing number of fast-food franchises.

As with any cosmopolitan city, dining out can be as simple as a bowl of noodles at a stand-up bar, to a five-star meal in a high-rise restaurant overlooking the city. Prices can range from 4,000 won (about $4 U.S.) for a no-frills meal, to more than 75,000 won (about $75 U.S.) for an opulent multi-course dinner. As in Japan, department stores feature in-house restaurants in their basements and on their upper floors. And if you're feeling really adventurous, duck down an alleyway and dine with the locals.

What to Do While You're There

The Palaces

Once a residential area reserved for Korean nobility and royalty, Pukch'on, the historic district, is located in the central and northern part of the city. Beginning at Kyongbokkung Station, a walk through this district and a tour of Kyongbokkung Palace takes about an hour. Ch'angdokkung Palace is the home of the reigning royal family, and is open to the public via guided tour. Although some of the grounds are off limits, it's worth the visit just to see the secret garden of Piwon, along with nearly 80 acres of landscapes graced with scenic ponds and pavilions. And as legend has it, passing under the Pullomun Gate will grant you eternal youth. Two other palaces of note are Toksugung, the smallest palace in Seoul, and Ch'anggyonggung, the oldest of Seoul's palaces. Both are worth a visit.

Shopping

The area around Samch'ongdonggil is lined with teashops and galleries that exhibit the works of local artists. And Seoul's It'aewon district is the shoppers' paradise you've no doubt heard so much about. With everything from souvenirs to designer knock-off's, it's the place to buy *omiyage* for all your friends back in Japan.

Other Attractions

To get up and above it all, Seoul Tower, one of the tallest in the world, features an observation deck and revolving restaurant. The tower also includes an Aquarium, the Ocean Life Museum, Funny World, a Game Room and the Natural Stone Exhibit. Namsan Park, which surrounds Seoul Tower is the site of the Botanical Gardens, the War Memorial, and the ruins of the ancient city walls.

Information Online

The Metropolitan Government of Seoul has a well designed website filled with general information on the city's main attractions and transit system to aid visitors to the city. You won't get the inside scoop on all the hot spots or out-of-the-way places to eat or stay, but there's lots of useful information there. **www.metro.seoul.kr/intro.html**

Lonely Planet Guide

www.lonelyplanet.com
Use the destination search engine to find good basic travelers' information on the city of Seoul. While you're there, check out the travelers' reports at **http://www.lonelyplanet.com/letters/nea/kor_pc.htm#Visa** for the inside scoop from those who have been there.

Rough Guides
www.roughguides.com
The information on this site has a genuine first-hand feel, with much more detail than the generic fluff that some other travel web sites pass off as inside information.

You're Free and Clear...For a Year

Once you receive your work visa, it's only good for a year. Recently however, the Japanese Ministry of Foreign Affairs has been issuing extended work visas for up to three years. Either way, your visa will eventually need to be renewed. This can be done at the Immigration Office from within Japan, and therefore does not require another trip to Seoul. However, to ensure continuity, it is important that you initiate the visa renewal process well in advance of the date your current visa expires.

Traveling Outside Japan During Your Residency

While you are residing in Japan, if you want to take a trip outside the country to visit home or to travel to some exotic vacation spot, you'll have to apply for a re-entry permit. You won't be allowed back in the country without it. So be sure to get one if you plan to travel. Permits for unlimited departures and re-entries are available for ¥6000 at the Japan Immigration Office. Single or double re-entries cost a little less. And when you do go to the Immigration Office, be sure to bring along something to read. You never know when two hundred and seventeen people might be in line ahead of you.

Visa Information on the World Wide Web

The Japanese Ministry of Foreign Affairs maintains a website www.mofa.go.jp/j_info/visit/visa/index.html with complete instructions and printable forms for obtaining all types of visas. The information it contains is simple, straightforward, easily accessible and expertly translated.

Notes:

Teaching English

Some schools provide a highly developed set of textbooks and teaching materials, and follow a strictly prescribed curriculum. Others rely on their teachers to design the curriculum and develop their own teaching materials. Many expect a little of both. This is also a consideration when deciding whether to take a teaching position at a particular school. Are you the type of teacher who follows rules and likes everything pre-planned? Or would you prefer to make things up spontaneously as you go along? Either way, there is an enormous variety of textbooks, supplemental resources, and highly effective techniques for teaching English to Japanese students.

Using Company Materials

Most reputable schools have a supply of textbooks and supplemental teaching materials available for teachers to use during lessons. These materials are designed and calibrated for the fluency level of each student, from absolute beginners to near-fluent speakers. In a well-developed curriculum, the core textbook will contain a set of sequential lessons designed to help the student build fluency, as well as a variety of supplemental teaching materials, such as games and puzzles, conversation starters, role-playing exercises, and visual aids. Most students who seek conversation lessons are more interested in practicing their speaking skills than working through a structured exercise. Therefore, a short grammatical exercise, followed by a related activity using supplemental materials correlated to the lesson, will allow the student to practice the grammatical structures in a fun and useful way, thereby reinforcing the focus of the lesson.

The Serendipitous Sensei

Certain smaller schools and company classes, as well as any private students you may have, will rely on you to design and produce each lesson. While this can be far more inspiring and enjoyable than following a prescribed textbook, producing a series of effective, interesting and entertaining lessons requires extra creativity and preparation time. Therefore, if you accept such a position, you will need your own supply of textbooks and supplemental teaching materials. As you will soon discover, there are hundreds of textbooks on the market, along with thousands of supplemental texts, from picture books to puzzle books, and everything in between.

The Frugal Sensei

Assembling your own set of teaching materials doesn't necessarily mean emptying your bank account. Once you've decided on a good basic grammar text, you need only one copy of the textbook for each fluency level, usually no more than three to five volumes. From these textbooks, you can make photocopied handouts of the lesson to give to each student in your group. This works well because the students can write directly on the lesson sheet and use it to take notes.

Beyond the basic grammar texts, a variety of games, puzzles, discussion prompts, and picture books is essential. But again, they needn't be costly. In fact, some of the best language teaching supplements cost little or nothing at all. When creatively employed, short newspaper and magazine articles, comic strips, crossword puzzles, advertisements and photographs provide excellent enhancements for the basic lesson. Games you may have enjoyed as a child, such as Twenty Questions, Hangman, I Spy, and Gossip can also be a great way to liven up a lesson.

Create Your Own Games

You can also come up with your own games. With little or no artistic talent, you can create a photocopied game template to play with your students. For example, here's a little game I came up with for helping beginner students with vocabulary building and answering basic questions. I call it The Suitcase Game:

On the top half of a plain sheet of paper, draw a picture of a suitcase with the lid open for packing. Fill the suitcase with about two dozen blank lines for writing a list of items one might take on a trip. On the bottom half of the page, make a list of travel questions with blank lines for answers. The list should include the questions: Where are you going on your trip? How will you travel (plane, car, train, bus)? How long will you stay? What time of year will you go? Is the trip for business or pleasure? What kinds of activities will your trip include? How much will the trip cost?

The Suitcase Game can be played as a group, or individually. The object of the game is to create a fantasy trip and fill the suitcase with all the items a traveler might need. As a follow-up exercise, ask the students to write a short travel log of the imaginary trip as if they had already taken it, complete with descriptions of the scenery, the hotel, the activities, the food, and the weather.

Another vocabulary-building game is one I call Categories A to Z. This game can be played on paper or in a conversation circle. To start, the teacher or one of the students chooses a category such as Countries, Food, Fruits & Vegetables, Animals, Furniture, Clothing, Colors, etc. The object of the game is to name an item in the category that begins with each letter of the alphabet.

Other Good Teaching Supplements

Depending on the level of your students, there are many other kinds of books besides textbooks that can be used to create interesting English lessons. One of my favorite types for any level are children's books that tell a story using only pictures, no text. This encourages students to come up with the words to tell the story themselves. And the more whimsical, the better. My favorites are:

The Snowman, by Raymond Briggs (New York : Random House, c1978.), in which a young boy is visited in the night by the snowman he built that afternoon, and the two show each other their worlds.

Two books by Caldecott Medal Winner David Wiesner: *Tuesday* (New York : Clarion Books, c1991.), in which frogs rise from their pond on lily pads and float through the air to explore the neighborhood;

and *Free Fall* (New York : Lothrop, Lee & Shepard Books, c1988.) in which a young boy dreams of an adventure in a magical land where the imaginary creatures he meets along the way are actually things in his bedroom that have come to life.

And another, *What's Silly*, by Niki Yektai illustrated by Susannah Ryan. (New York : Clarion Books, c1989.) in which each page contains an illustration of a family in various everyday situations, but with something amiss in each, for example, cars driving on water and boats on the road, shoes in the sink and dishes on the children's feet.

The delightful illustrations on every page of these books offer excellent opportunities for students to practice sentence structure and vocabulary (especially verbs). Of course, these are only a few of the hundreds of beautifully illustrated books that can serve as a creative venue for learning.

Another technique for intermediate and advanced students is to use Japanese translations of well-known books such as *Alice in Wonderland* by Lewis Carroll; *The Little Prince*, by Antoine de St. Exupéry; and *Winnie the Pooh*, by A.A. Milne. Most students are quite familiar with these titles, and the task of translating a passage from one of them back to English, can be both challenging and enjoyable.

For something a little more fun and "hands on," fill a paper bag with a dozen or more common household objects, such as a clothespin, a comb, a coin, a hair accessory, a scouring pad, a battery, a spoon, and other small, safe items from around the house. Have your student reach into the bag and grasp an object. Without taking it out of the bag, have the student describe its qualities (round, pointed, metal, wooden, rough, soft, etc.), and if they can identify it by touch only, have them describe what the object is used for. This can even be a guessing game to be played with the group. If there's time left at the end of the lesson, or for a homework assignment, have each student choose an object and write a paragraph about it.

It's Right Under Your Nose

As you can see, an English lesson can be created from almost anything, and teaching opportunities are literally everywhere. All it takes is a little creativity to come up with a way to apply and present it. So if you find yourself stumped for a lesson, just open your eyes and look around you.

Determining the Value of a Lesson

A good rule of thumb to use when evaluating the value of a lesson is to ask yourself, "If the tables were turned and I were the student, would I be interested in learning this lesson in Japanese?" Remember that as a native speaker of English, you may take for granted the simple things that constitute everyday verbal communication. Yet everyday phrases, idiomatic expressions and pop culture references are the very things that students crave. With a little imagination, you can find or create captivating language-teaching games and supplements of your own to spice up any lesson and teach your students the things they really want to learn.

Resources on the World Wide Web

A simple keyword search, using "ESL books" or "ESL teaching ideas," will yield dozens of results. Here are two of the best:

Textbooks

Alta Book Center **www.altaesl.com** is the largest source of ESL books and materials in the world. They carry thousands of titles on grammar, culture, teaching techniques, workbooks, games, videos, specialized vocabulary, dictionaries, and books on teaching English in specific countries. These titles are available for ordering on the website using e-mail, phone, fax, or postal mail. You can also order a hard copy of their catalog for free within the U.S. For catalogues to countries outside of North America and Mexico, there is a shipping charge of $8.00, which can be applied as credit towards your purchase. Therefore it might be wise to order one of their catalogs to take with you to Japan. Alta Book Center can be contacted by Email: info@altaesl.com .Fax: 800 ALTA/FAX or 650.692.4654, Phone: 800 ALTA/ESL or 650.692.1285, or Mail: Alta Books, 14 Adrian Court, Burlingame, California 94010 USA.

ESL Resources and Teaching Ideas

Dave's ESL Café **www.eslcafe.com** This multi-cultural website provides dozens of useful features, including an extensive bookstore, a forum, a job board, a chat room, teachers' journals, a help line, and best of all, hundreds of clever teaching ideas to help you prepare fun, interesting and effective lessons.

Notes:

Survival Tips

Making the decision to pull up stakes and move to the other side of the planet is a significant life choice that will transform you and shape your destiny in countless ways. And whether the experience is a triumph or a fiasco will depend largely on how well you prepare and adapt. Unless you are a loner by nature, one of the most important things you can do to ensure the quality of your life in Japan is to get yourself connected to a wide variety of people. In addition to socializing after hours with the teaching staff at the company where you work, getting to know the natives can be a uniquely meaningful and rewarding part of your experience. The Japanese people are remarkably hospitable and welcoming. And because they are always eager to practice their English in everyday life, you may be approached by total strangers who will strike up a conversation in a public place and eventually invite you to go with them to a *kisaten* for coffee, or to nearby *izakaya* for snacks and drinks. If and when this happens, as long as it's in a reputable, well-lit and populated neighborhood, it's quite acceptable and safe to say yes. Just be sure to use your intuition and common sense when agreeing to get involved with strangers.

Getting to know your neighbors and the proprietors of small businesses in your neighborhood is another way to make personal contacts in Japan. In fact, it is customary in certain places to exchange small welcome gifts with your neighbors. Gifts of food or small personal items such as handkerchiefs or stationery make a nice introductory gesture. In your immediate neighborhood, there are also numerous opportunities to interact with the locals at the market, the convenience store, the dry cleaner, and the post office. Most neighborhoods also have a modest little eating establishment with friendly owners who welcome regular patrons. This is a perfect setting in which to get acquainted, to learn the language and the culture up close, and to cultivate a sense of belonging.

In addition to immersing yourself in the local habitat, here is a list of other simple suggestions that will make your stay in Japan more pleasant and comfortable.

Learn to speak and read as much of the language as you can before you go.

As you become acclimated to your surroundings and begin to interact with the Japanese people, you will, no doubt, feel the unique kind of frustration that a lack of vocabulary and language skills can produce. Therefore, if you have a basic grasp of the language when you arrive, you can immediately begin building upon that foundation and find yourself well on your way toward fluency.

Carry a pocket dictionary with you at all times.

You will need it practically every minute of the day when you first arrive, especially when shopping and asking directions. Carrying a dictionary will also allow you enjoy a little basic conversation in social settings. Here's a hint: If there's a word you need that isn't in your dictionary, ask someone how to say it in Japanese and jot it down on the inside cover or on the empty pages in the back.

Carry a small notepad and keep notes.

When you first arrive in Japan, you'll be inundated with all kinds of new information. So it's a good idea to keep a notebook handy for jotting down people's names, directions to homes and offices, the names and locations of shops and restaurants that you like, the names of interesting places to visit on your days off, new words or phrases you want to remember, and other interesting facts about Japan.

Make arrangements for any prescription drugs you must take regularly.

Medical practices in Japan differ somewhat from those in the U.S., and there are also certain restrictions on both prescription and over-the-counter medications. Recreational narcotics and stimulants are strictly prohibited and as a result, all pharmaceutical substances are closely monitored. Travelers are only allowed a two-month's supply of over-the-counter medications, and a one-month's supply of prescription drugs (which must be accompanied by a copy of the prescription). And even as recently as 1999, oral contraceptives were unavailable in Japan, but have since been approved for general distribution. So if you have a need for regular medication of any kind, get a copy of your prescription from your doctor and place the task of finding a physician in Japan at the top of your list.

If you are larger than average in size, pack a box of extra clothes and shoes to ship by surface mail once you have a permanent address.
As a people, the Japanese tend to be smaller in stature than the average American. Therefore, if you are considered large, or even medium in size, you may have trouble buying clothing off the rack, and shoes that fit may be especially hard to find. So it's a wise idea to pack yourself a box of spare clothes and shoes for the upcoming seasons.

If you wear glasses or contact lenses, bring an extra pair or supply.
As with everything else in Japan, eyewear is prohibitively expensive. So bring along a spare, and if possible, get your eyes checked and your lenses upgraded just before you leave. That way, you'll be good for at least a year.

Get some waterproof shoes for both winter and summer wear.
On the island of Honshu, the seasons in Japan tend to be rainy for much of the warmer months; and in the winter, which tends to be mild and dry, expect the occasional snowfall. And since the daily business of commuting to work will probably entail walking to and from the train station, a couple of pairs of waterproof shoes will be a godsend on wet days. For winter, a pair of fleece-lined boots will keep your feet warm and dry as you trudge through the slush that's leftover after light snow. And in the summer, a pair of watertight walking shoes is your best bet. But when it comes to athletic shoes, many schools and companies prohibit such casual footwear in their dress codes, so be sure to choose plain, stylish-looking ones that would not be categorized as "sneakers." That way you'll be able to wear them to work without having to change into another pair when you arrive. If your job requires something more upscale in the way of footwear, then you may have to keep a pair at work, or carry them to work with you on rainy days.

Fill your summer wardrobe with loose-fitting cotton clothing.
The Japanese have a word for the summer climate, and that word is
mushi-atsui. It literally means "steamy hot." There's really no
antidote for it except air conditioning. However, a wardrobe of lightweight, loose-fitting, natural fiber garments will provide the best
measure of comfort when you have to be outdoors.

**Pack some small items in your
luggage to give as hospitality gifts.**
The Japanese people love to give gifts. They have two special
seasons, one in summer and one in winter, which are dedicated to
gift giving. Throughout the rest of the year, gifts are exchanged on
almost every occasion, and at other times, for no reason at all. When
you arrive, you will meet many people who will help you in some
way, and although it's not expected, a small token of appreciation
will go a long way toward endearing you to your hosts, neighbors
and employers. These gifts needn't be expensive or elaborate. Small
items such as American cigarettes, cigars and whiskey, sealed
gourmet food items, music tapes and CD's, movie DVD's & videos,
small accessories with designer logos on them, stationery, attractive
books, and pop culture items make perfect gifts for adults, and
comic books and small toys are good gifts for children. So be sure to
squirrel away a few such items in your luggage to bestow on your
hosts, employers, landlords and new acquaintances at opportune times.

Laminate a small transit map and carry it with you.
The transit system in Japan, and especially in Tokyo can be confusing
for a number of reasons. Many if not most of the signs are written in
Japanese, and the various transit lines crisscross each other like a
giant plate of spaghetti. So until you're familiar with the train and
subway system, it's a good idea to carry a small transit map with you
when you're out and about. Mine was a scaled-down version, with a
map of the city on one side, and an abstract of the train lines on the
other. It fit perfectly in a sturdy clear plastic cover that I purchased
at the local stationery store and kept tucked away in my briefcase.
That simple item was a lifesaver on more than one occasion.

Buy a monthly rail pass, along with a little plastic sleeve to keep it in, and carry it with you at all times.

The best way to travel locally is by train. And chances are, your employer will reimburse you each month for a rail pass for travel between the school or company, and the station where you live. These passes can be purchased for up to a year, however after only a few weeks, left unprotected they can become quite dog-eared. Almost everyone in Japan carries a rail pass and therefore, there is quite a thriving market for little sleeves to keep them undamaged for the duration of their use. These rail pass covers can be bought at department stores, sundries shops and station platform kiosks.

Write down the directions to your job and your apartment.

When you get hired and find a place to live, you will have to memorize the routes to them from the train station to keep from getting lost for the first few days. Smaller streets in Japan do not typically have signs, or even names for that matter. So it's a good idea to write down a description of the streets you must take to get there and include especially conspicuous landmarks.

Carry tissues with you at all times.

Oddly enough, in a culture known for its etiquette and hygiene, there may be times when you find yourself in need of a napkin and there's none to be had. This can happen in restaurants, restrooms, trains, cinemas, and any number of other public places. Fortunately, one of the most common forms of mass marketing in Japan is corporate advertising printed on little packages of tissues, which *arubaito* workers distribute to passers by on city streets.

Exchange books and magazines with your fellow teachers and friends.

Once you're settled in Japan, you'll soon find that entertainment in a language you can understand is both scarce and expensive. It costs a fortune to go to the cinema, and for your money you're not always guaranteed a seat with your ticket purchase. For home entertainment, there are only a couple of television stations that broadcast English movies, usually in the wee hours of the morning; and buying a VCR and renting videos can also be pricey. So you may find yourself turning to books as a way to occupy your mind in the evenings. But like every other imported commodity in Japan, a garden-variety paperback book can cost upwards of ¥1500 at Kinokuniya Bookstore. Because of this, ex-pats in Japan tend to form book-swapping circles. They're informal and work on the honor system. If you have a book or magazine that you're finished with, you can trade it for another with one of your neighbors or co-workers. Of course, you can't be choosey, because taste in reading material varies from one individual to the next. So you may eventually even find yourself reading police procedurals and bodice rippers. But after a while, you'll be grateful for *anything* in English. So the motto is: Read it and pass it along. What goes around comes around.

Go on day trips to nearby sites.

Once you're settled, begin exploring places that you can reach by train within a few minutes or even a couple of hours on your days off. Regardless of which region you choose to call home, each has its own charms and scenic attractions, from parks and gardens, to museums and historic treasures. Even in the most urban of cities, every district has its own shrine or temple with a background of historic significance. Ask your students for recommendations and directions.

Buy a bicycle.

This is one of the best modes of transportation in Japan. Not only are they inexpensive, they are also fully sanctioned for riding on city streets and sidewalks. A bicycle will greatly facilitate your trip to and from the train station every day, not to mention errands and recreational outings. There are limitations to the virtues of a bicycle however. The metropolitan train stations have limited areas for bicycle parking, yet on busy weekdays, the racks and lamp posts and fence posts surrounding the station are thronged with bicycles, so there's often no place to lock and leave yours while you're away at work. In some cases, illegally parked bicycles are impounded. And even with a lock, bicycle theft is still common. Never rely solely on the wheel lock that comes as a standard feature on most models. Lock your bike with a sturdy chain, and even then, don't be surprised if you find it missing when you return from work one day. But don't let that stop you from buying one. You'll be glad you did. Just be mindful of where and how you park it.

Keep several umbrellas handy at home, at work, and in your briefcase.

Between the annual rainy season, the typhoon season, and the occasional snowstorm, residents of Japan have a perpetual need for umbrellas. And due to the unpredictable nature of the weather, a sudden rainstorm can occur at any time. On any given day, it may be clear and sunny when you leave home, and pouring buckets by the time you're ready to head home. So it's always a good idea to keep a folding umbrella with you during the inclement seasons, as well as a spare at work and at home. But again, don't be surprised when one of them turns up missing. You never know when a perfectly innocent yet umbrella-bereft person will "borrow" yours and permanently forget to return it.

Ask your friends and family to send you comfort items and fun stuff.

Once you have a permanent address, you can receive packages from home. In addition to the surface mail package that you prepared before you left, you can ask your family to send you books, toiletries, clothes, tapes, CD's and personal mementos. Depending what's in the package, buying and shipping these items from the U.S. can be less expensive than purchasing them in Japan.

Buy Aerograms for writing letters to friends and family.

For those of you who have never seen an aerogram, it's a clever little self-contained correspondence sheet that can be written on, folded and mailed as a single unit without a stamp or an envelope. They're lightweight, less expensive than stamps and envelopes, and you can get them at the post office.

Update your address book and print out several sheets of address labels.

Once you're living in Japan, you may want to correspond with friends and family. If you're not set up for e-mail, then you will have to resort to the old-fashioned postal method instead. A handy way to make it easy to prepare letters and aerograms for mailing is to make up a set of pre-printed, self-adhesive labels on your home computer for those friends and family members you'll be corresponding with while you're away. Just calculate how often you think you'll write letters, and print up that many address labels for each person.

Watch out for automatic taxi doors.

One of the peculiarities of Japanese taxicabs is a clever little device that allows the driver to open the back doors of the cab from the driver's seat. If you don't know to expect it, you can get broadsided by the rear passenger door as it flies open to let you in. So be forewarned and stand back.

Get in the habit of double-checking the traffic in both directions before crossing the street.

Drivers in Japan keep to the left on all highways and city streets, which can be a little disorienting when you first arrive if you're used to the opposite convention. And there are many one-way streets. So for the sake of self-preservation get in the habit of looking both ways before crossing.

Use a sleep mask in the summer months.

Japan does not observe Daylight Savings Time in the spring and summer months. This means that as the declination of the sun increases, the sunrise occurs earlier and earlier each day. Around the time of the summer solstice, it's not unusual to see the glow of dawn creep over the horizon and hear the mocking "Haa-haa" of the blackbirds as they take flight, sometimes as early as 3:30 a.m. So if you have trouble sleeping after sunrise, wear a sleep mask to be sure you get a full night's rest.

Ask your employer not to withhold Social Security.

Some employers deduct social security taxes from your paychecks. However, in some cases, they are not required to do so, and therefore you may request that they do not. Under the current law, foreigners must pay Social Security taxes for 25 years before they can collect any benefits. But in the event that your employer insists on withholding Social Security, a new law allows a refund of up to three years' withholdings upon your departure from Japan.

Enroll in the National Health Plan.

Unlike the U.S., all Japanese workers are covered by some kind of health insurance. It's mandatory. Even foreign workers are sometimes included in the company's health insurance plan. However, if your employer does not offer health insurance benefits, once you complete your Alien Registration, you must enroll in the National

Health Plan. This health insurance plan is provided by the local wards to cover self-employed workers, and those people who are not otherwise eligible for private health insurance. When you apply for the National Health Plan at your ward office, you will be issued a health insurance card that covers 70% of all medical treatment.

Don't spend more than 35 days a year visiting the U.S.

The U.S. tax law states that an American citizen earning money in a foreign country for 330 days out of a consecutive 365 days is exempt from income taxes. The consecutive days can be from any calendar date to the same day on the following year, for example March first to March first. Your days outside the country do not have to be consecutive however. They just have to total 330 in any fiscal year. If your stay outside of the country does not meet the required minimum, you will be required to pay income tax and social security tax based on self-employment rates. Employers in Japan do not typically report your income to the IRS, but transactions such as wiring money to your bank account or exchanging yen for dollars all leave a paper trail.

Notes:

Cultural Do's & Don'ts

**Never poke chopsticks into your food
and leave them standing upright in it.**
As innocent as it may sound, this is one of the most offensive things
you can do in polite company in Japan. The horror associated with
this faux pas comes from the tradition of making food offerings to
the dead at burial sites on those occasions that honor the souls of
the dearly departed. An offering of rice for the deceased is placed in
a bowl on the gravesite with a pair of chopsticks standing upright in it.

Don't pass food from one pair of chopsticks to another.
There's an ancient custom in Japan that is related to the funeral
ceremony. After the cremation, family members pass the charred
remains of the deceased from the crematory chamber to the funereal
urn with chopsticks. It's a social blunder to do so with food.

**Don't pick up food from a shared plate with the end
of the chopsticks that has been in your mouth.**
For obvious reasons, turn them around and use the other end to
pick up the food and put it on your plate. Also, never point at
anyone or anything with your chopsticks, don't use them to spear a
morsel of food, and don't wave them around in the air or use them
to gesture while you're talking. It's bad etiquette.

**In social settings, never pour your own beverage,
and always offer to pour beverages for others.**
The Japanese have a tradition of pouring each other's beverages
when sharing from a common container such as a teapot, beer bottle
or sake carafe. So unless you're drinking alone, don't fill your own

glass. Instead, when yours is empty, reach out and fill someone else's glass. They will notice that yours needs refilling too and reciprocate.

Mind your *shi's* and *ku's*.

Shi and *Ku*, the Japanese words for four and nine, also happen to be phonetically identical to the words for death and pain. Therefore, they are considered unlucky numbers. Some hospitals and other buildings do not have a fourth or ninth floor, and goods that come in sets avoid those numbers as well. When counting in Japanese, the word *yon* is often substituted for *shi*; and *shichi*, the word for seven, is often changed to the more benign word *nana*. So mind your *shi's* and *ku's*.

Left over Right.

If you have occasion to wear a *yukata*, *hanten* or *kimono*, be sure to wrap the front opening left over right. Right over left is strictly for corpses. It's a small detail, but the Japanese take notice of these little things.

Offer your seat to elderly, pregnant or handicapped people on trains and buses.

You'll be riding trains almost every day, and this one is just common courtesy in any country. The Japanese themselves don't always do it, but you should anyway.

Keep to the left when walking.

As with driving, the convention in Japan is to keep to the left. If forgotten, you will undoubtedly find yourself dodging a steady stream of oncoming pedestrians headed in the opposite direction.

Always address adults with the respectful suffix "–san" until you establish very friendly and familiar terms.

Despite their friendly nature, the Japanese maintain a certain social distance, especially in the early stages of friendship. The customary form of address is to add the suffix "san" to the end of the surname. So, for example, Mr. Takeda should be referred to as Takeda-san, unless you are instructed to refer to that person by a first name or a nickname.

Don't pat children on the head or touch them in any other way unless you know it's okay to do so.
Japanese children are adorable, and the urge to touch them in some affectionate way can be tempting. However, it is considered impolite to make physical contact with a child unless you are well acquainted with the family.

Don't hug or kiss anyone unless you absolutely know it's okay.
Physical contact in social situations in Japan is taboo, except in very familiar circumstances. The tradition of bowing as a form of greeting is still widely practiced, and even a simple handshake is reserved for international business greetings. And hugs or kisses will cause extreme awkwardness except in the most familiar circumstances.

Don't let anyone see you yawn.
Although it is a natural human phenomenon, yawning is considered very rude in Japan, especially during a lesson. Therefore, for the sake of etiquette, it is important that you learn to stifle a yawn.

Don't stare at people.
Staring in any culture is impolite, however, it is especially so in Japan. One of the ways that this enormous population is able to coexist peacefully in such overcrowded cities is by giving each other personal space and a certain measure of anonymity and invisibility. As a result, you may see people doing some pretty offensive things in public places, but if you stare at them and get disgusted, then it's considered your own fault for looking.

Always remove your shoes at the door of homes and even some businesses, unless otherwise indicated.
Because *tatami* mats and other kinds of floors are still used as surfaces for sitting at low tables and sleeping on futons, the age-old tradition of removing shoes at the door is still widely practiced throughout all of Japan. Get used to the custom, and choose a shoe style that is easy to remove when you arrive and to put back on again when you leave. And when you do take them off, place them neatly side by side with the toes pointing toward the door.

Watch and Learn

One of the simplest and best cultural survival tips of all is to simply pay attention. Watch and learn. Observe the actions and behavior of others, and don't overlook the smallest detail. And as trite as it may sound, this variation on a well-known proverb will serve you well: "When in Japan, do as the Japanese do."

Notes:

_____

_____

_____

_____

_____

_____

_____

_____

_____

_____

_____

_____

_____

_____

_____

_____

_____

_____

_____

_____

_____

_____

_____

_____

_____

Resources, Bibliography, Webliography & Glossary

Books
Language
Webster's New World Compact J/E-E/J Dictionary. For a good, all-around portable, it's the best of the bunch.

Let's Learn Hiragana and *Let's Learn Katakana*, and *Let's Learn Kanji*, by Yasuko Mitamura. Good beginner's texts for learning the three alphabets of the Japanese language.

Japanese in 10 Minutes a Day, by Kristine K. Kershul. A highly effective program for gaining a good grasp of basic Japanese that will serve you well when you first arrive in Japan.

Making Out In Japanese, by Todd and Erica Geer. This little phrasebook contains everyday expressions that you won't find in dictionaries and textbooks; phrases to help you with casual chatting, handling yourself with conflicts, and even the language of romance.

History and Culture
Passport's Japan Almanac by Boye de Mente. Japanese culture A to Z. Currently out of print, but well worth tracking down a used copy.

The Chrysanthemum and the Sword by Ruth Benedict. The classic historical and authoritative text on the evolution and ideology of the Japanese culture.

You Gotta Have Wa, by Robert Whiting. Using the game of baseball as a metaphor, Whiting examines the underlying concepts of harmony and the hive mentality in Japan.

Personal Narrative

36 Views of Mt Fuji, by Cathy Davidson. An insightful and revealing examination of the many layered and faceted Japanese way, leads the author to hold a mirror up to her own life.

Dave Barry Does Japan, by Dave Barry. The endearing eccentricities of the Japanese people and their culture lampooned as only Dave Barry can.

Learning to Bow, by Bruce S. Feiler. An insider's perspective on living and working in Japan by a seasoned JET vet.

Lost Japan, by Alex Kerr. An award-winning overview of the changing face of Japan that encompasses three decades of the author's residency.

The Accidental Office Lady, by Laura Kriska. A look at the corporate world of Japan through the eyes of an author who is not only foreign, but also female. A fresh perspective after all the books written about teaching English from a male point of view.

The Lady and the Monk: Four Seasons in Kyoto. Acclaimed travel writer Pico Iyer recounts his life in Kyoto, which started out as the aesthetic adventure of a would-be ascetic, and evolved into an enlightening relationship with both a Japanese woman and with Japan itself.

The Roads to Sata, by Alan Booth. A remarkable journal by a man who walked the entire length of Japan. An excellent choice once you're familiar with the culture and geography.

Travel Guides

Fodor's Japan. Always a colorful and trustworthy companion.

Lonely Planet Japan. An excellent travel guide.

Fiction

Black Rain, by Masuji Ibuse. A poignant account of the bombing of Hiroshima and its impact on the lives of ordinary people.

Botchan, *Kokoro*, and *I Am A Cat* by Natsume Soseki. Three classics by Japan's most beloved author.

Kitchen, by Banana Yoshimoto. Contemporary fiction about a young girl's quest to find a place to call home, both in the world, and in her heart.

Memoirs of a Geisha, by Arthur Golden. This best-selling work of historical fiction meticulously captures the hidden world of the Geisha with impressive authenticity and detail.

Movies

Tampopo - One woman's search for the perfect bowl of noodles. Directed by Juzo Itami.

A Taxing Woman – An amusing peek inside contemporary Japan through the eyes of a Japanese tax collector. Directed by Juzo Itami.

The Funeral – A dark yet amusing satire of life, death and love. Directed by Juzo Itami.

Seven Samurai – The quintessential Japanese classic. You will no doubt recognize this one as the basis for the American western *The Magnificent Seven*. Be forewarned however: it's long, it's subtitled, and it's filmed in black and white. But excellent nonetheless. Directed by Akira Kurosawa.

Shogun – Based on the novel by James Clavell, this westernized interpretation of feudal Japan offers entertainment in epic proportions. Directed by Jerry London.

Totoro – Magic is afoot in this charming tale of two girls whose family has moved to the countryside for their mother's recuperation from an illness. Japanese animation at its best. Directed by Hayao Miyazaki.

A List of Internet Web sites Mentioned in the Text

For your convenience, the following links are also listed on the Ganbatte web page. Instead of typing each URL into your browser, you can access all the websites mentioned in this book at **http://www.thingsasian.com/ganbatte**

Alta Book Center: **www.altaesl.com/**

Amazon.com: **www.amazon.com/**

Ask Dr. Weil: **www.askdrweil.com/**

Best Fares: **www.bestfares.com/**

Career Cross Japan: **www.careercross.com/**

City of Fukuoka Website: **www.city.fukuoka.jp/**

City of Hiroshima Website: **www.city.hiroshima.jp/**

City of Kanazawa Website:
www.city.kanazawa.ishikawa.jp/kanazawaE.html

City of Kawasaki Website: **www.city.kawasaki.jp/**

City of Kitakyushu Website: **www.city.kitakyushu.jp/**

City of Kobe Website: **www.city.kobe.jp/**

City of Kyoto Website: **www.city.kyoto.jp/**

City of Matsuyama Website: **www.city.matsuyama.ehime.jp/**

City of Nagasaki Website:
www-cc.nagasaki-u.ac.jp/nagasaki-city/nagasaki.html

City of Nagoya Website: **www.city.nagoya.jp/**

City of Osaka Website: **www.city.osaka.jp/**

City of SapporoWebsite: **www.city.sapporo.jp/**

City of Sendai Website: **www.city.sendai.jp/**

City of Seoul Website: **www.metro.seoul.kr/intro.html**

City of Takamatsu Website: **www.city.takamatsu.kagawa.jp/**

City of Tokyo Website: **www.tcvb.or.jp/**

City of Yokohama Website: **www.city.yokohama.jp/**

Dave's ESL Café: **www.eslcafe.com/**

Discovery.com website: **http://www.discovery.com/**

Escape Artist: **www.escapeartist.com/**

Embassy of Japan: **www.embjapan.org/**

Embassy World: **www.embassyworld.com**

Gaijin Pot: **www.gaijinpot.com/**

Interac: **www.interac.co.jp/recruit**

International Tourist Center of Japan: **www.itcj.or.jp/**

Internet service providers: **http://thelist.internet.com/countrycode/81/**

Japan Helpline: **www.jhelp.com**

Japan Information Network: **http://jin.jcic.or.jp/**

Japan Times Overseas Subscriptions: **overseas@japantimes.co.jp.**

Japan Times Website: **www.japantimes.co.jp/**

Japan Youth Hostels, Inc.: **www.jyh.or.jp/**

Japanese Customs Information: **www.mof.go.jp/~customs/fvisit-e.htm**

Japanese Department of State Customs Information:
http://travel.state.gov/japan.html

Japanese LanguageTutorials: **www.findtutorials.com/**

Japanese Ministry of Foreign Affairs website:
www.mofa.go.jp/j_info/visit/visa/index.html

Japanorama: www.japanorama.com/

JET Alumni Association Handbook:
www.jetaasc.org/php/index.php?index=handbook

JET Article on using a computer in Japan:
www.jetaasc.org/php/article.php?content=computers

Jim Breen's Japanese Page:
www.csse.monash.edu.au/~jwb/japanese.html

Jobs in Japan: www.jobsinjapan.com/

Kimi Information Center: www2.dango.ne.jp/kimi/index.html

Legend of Hachiko:
www.metropolis.co.jp/biginjapanarchive349/303/biginjapaninc.htm

Life in Tokyo: www.lifeintokyo.com

Live Door: www.livedoor.com/

Lonely Planet: www.lonelyplanet.com/

Lonely Planet Travelers' Reports:
www.lonelyplanet.com/letters/nea/kor_pc.htm#Visa

Luis Poza's Website: http://poza.net/japan/

Maps.com: www.maps.com/

My Yahoo: http://my.yahoo.com/

Narita Airport Customs Information: www.narita-airport-customs.go.jp/

NASA photo of Tokyo: http://earth.jsc.nasa.gov./

NTT Japan Window: www.jwindow.net/

Ohayo Sensei: www.ohayosensei.com/

Open Learning International: www.olionline.com/

Orbitz: **www.orbitz.com/**

Price Check Tokyo: **www.pricechecktokyo.com/**

Rough Guides: **www.roughguides.com**

Teaching English in Japan: **www.wizweb.com/~susan/japan**

TEFL.com: **www.tefl.com/**

The Japan FAQ Know Before You Go Website: **thejapanfaq.cjb.net**

The JET Alumni Association of Southern California: **www.jetaasc.org/**

The JET Program: **www.mofa.go.jp/j_info/visit/jet/index.html**

The TEFL Center: **www.teflcenter.com/**

Tokyo Classified: **www.tokyoclassified.com/**

Tokyo Globe: **www.tokyoglobe.com/**

U.S. Passport Information:
http://travel.state.gov/passport_services.html

Travelocity: **www.travelocity.com/**

U.S. Postal Service website: **http://www.usps.com/**

Vaccination Information: **www.cdc.gov/travel/vaccinat.htm**

Major Airlines to Japan and Seoul
Japan Airlines: **www.jal.co.jp/**
1-800-525-3663

Korean Airlines: **www.koreanair.com**
1-800-438-5000

American Airlines: **www.aa.com/**
1-800-433-7300

United Airlines: **www.ual.com/**
1-800-241-6522

Embassies & Consulates
The Japanese Embassy in the U.S.
2520 Massachusetts Avenue N.W.
Washington, D.C. 20008
(202) 238-6700

Japanese Consulates
Alabama
358 East Byron Avenue
Mobile, AL 36609
(334) 342-6654

Alaska
3601 C Street, Suite 1300,
Anchorage, AK 99503-5925
(907) 562-8424

Arizona
40 N. Central Avenue, Suite 2700
Phoenix, AZ 85004
(602) 528-4000

California
350 S. Grand Avenue, Suite 1700
Los Angeles, CA 90071
(213) 617-6700

10455 Pomerado Road
San Diego, CA 92131
(619) 635-4537

50 Fremont Street, Suite 2300
San Francisco, CA 94105
(415) 777-3533

Colorado
1225 17th Street, Suite 3000
Denver, CO 80202
(303) 534-1151

Connecticut
50 Tower Lane
Avon, CT 06001
(860) 677-9707

Florida
Brickwell Bay View Tower
80 S.W. 8th Street, Suite 3200
Miami, FL 33130.
(305) 530-9090

Georgia
100 Colony Square Building
1175 Peachtree Street N.E., Suite 2000
Atlanta, GA 30361.
(404) 892-2700

Guam
Guam International Trade Center Building
590 S. Marine Drive, Suite 604
Agana, Tamuning 96911

Hawaii
1742 Nuuanu Avenue
Honolulu, HI 96817
(808) 536-2226

Illinois
737 N. Michigan Avenue, Suite 1100
Chicago, IL 60611
(312) 280-0400

Japan Information Center
737 N. Michigan Avenue, Suite 1000
Chicago, IL 60611
(312) 280-0430

Indiana
11 S. Meridian Street
Indianapolis, IN 46204
(317) 231-7227

Louisiana
639 Loyola Avenue, Suite 2050
New Orleans, LA 70113
(504) 529-2101

Massachusetts
Federal Resesrve Plaza
600 Atlantic Avenue, 14th Floor
Boston, MA 02210.
(617) 973-9772

Michigan
400 Renaissance Center, Suite 1600
Detroit, MI 48243
(313) 567-0120

Minnesota
603 E. Lake Street
Wayzata
Minneapolis, MI 55391

Missouri
Commerce Tower
911 Main Street, Room 1800,
Kansas City, MO 64105.
(816) 471-0111

46 Briarcliff Street
St. Louis, MO 63124
(314) 994-1133

Nebraska
412 N. 85th Street
Omaha, NE 68114
(402) 399-0928

New York
85 Windsor Avenue
Buffalo, NY 14209
(716) 884-2376

New York cont.
299 Park Avenue, 18 & 19 Floor
New York, NY 10171
(212) 371-8222

North Carolina
305 W. High St., Suite 416
High Point, NC 27260

Ohio
1712 Neil Avenue, Suite 325
Columbus, OH 43210
(614) 292-3345

Oregon
Wells Fargo Center
1300 S.W. 5th Avenue, Suite 2700
Portland, OR 97201
(503) 221-1811

Pennsylvania
140 Jaffrey Road
Malvern
Philadelphia, PA 19355
(610) 644-4507

Puerto Rico
530 Ponce De Leon Avenue
San Juan, Puerto Rico 00902
(787) 722-0483

Tennessee
Nelson Capitol Corporation
3401 West End Building, Suite 300
Nashville, TN 37203
(615) 292-8787

Texas
7115 Fernmeadow Circle
Dallas, TX 75248
(972) 661-2346

Texas cont.
Wells Fargo Plaza
1000 Louisiana Street, Suite 5300
Houston, TX 77002
(713) 652-2977

Washington
601 Union Street, Suite 500
Seattle, WA 98101
(206) 682-9107

Wyoming
111 W. 14th Street
Casper, WY 82601
(307) 234-2317

Japanese Embassy Online
Embassy of Japan **www.embjapan.org/**

*Online links to Japan Consulates are also
available for the following cities:*

Anchorage: **www.embjapan.org/anchorage/**

Atlanta: **www.cgjapanatlanta.org/**

Boston: **www.embjapan.org/boston/**

Chicago: **www.jchicago.org/**

Denver: **www.embjapan.org/denver/**

Detroit: **www.embjapan.org/detroit/**

Honolulu: **www.embjapan.org/honolulu/**

Houston: **www.cgjhouston.org/**

Kansas City: **www.embjapan.org/kansascity/**

Los Angeles: **www.embjapan.org/la/**

Miami: **www.cgjapanmia.org/**

New Orleans: **www.embjapan.org/neworleans/**

New York: **http://ny.cgj.org/**

Portland: **www.embjapan.org/portland/**

San Francisco: **www.cgjsf.org/**

Seattle: **www.cgjapansea.org/**

Useful Telephone Numbers
Japan Helpline by Agape International
tel: 0990-54-0953 **www.jhelp.com** On the website, you can order
a wallet-sized card with emergency telephone numbers.

Police (throughout Japan)...110

Fire/Ambulance (throughout Japan)...119

Police / General Information (in Japanese)...03-3501-0110

Lost and Found (in Japanese) 03-3814-4151

Tokyo Metropolitan Police Department Counseling Service for
Foreigners 03-3503-8484

English Directory Assistance
Domestic Assistance : 104

International Assistance: 0057_

AMDA International Medical Information Center
Kanto Area 03-5285-8088

Kansai Area 06-6636-2333

Additional Help Online
Life in Tokyo
www.lifeintokyo.com

This website contains dozens of resources for information, emergency services, counseling, and general advice on getting by in Japan. It focuses mainly on the Tokyo Metropolitan area, however, there is also abundant information on Japan in general and links to resources in other areas of the country.

Creating a Dynamic Resume

Your resume is your ambassador to the employment world. It speaks for you in your absence. Therefore it is important for your resume to say the right things about you to prospective employers. The most important thing to remember is that those employers have seen a thousand resumes, and yours is just one more. So how are you going to make it stand out without resorting to pop-ups and perfume? Follow these surefire suggestions:

Formatting: Your resume should be clean, well organized, and unless you have a lengthy curriculum vitae, it should fit on a single page. Make sure your outline style is consistent and your alignment is uniform. Avoid the use of flashy stationery or elaborate fonts. Stick to something like Times New Roman or Arial on conservative, high-quality stationery and let the content of your resume speak for itself.

The Heading: Centered at the very top of your resume, your heading should include your name (in bold); your street address; your city, state and zip; your telephone number; your fax number (if you have one); and your e-mail address.

Your Objective: This element of your resume should be a single line that reads like a mission statement. Your objective line should clearly state what position you are applying for, what you hope to achieve and how you plan to advance in that capacity.

Your Qualifications: Here's where you get to brag about yourself (but only a little). Compose a few concise lines describing why the company should hire you. These qualities can include your outgoing and enthusiastic personality, your extensive experience, your knowledge of Japanese culture and language, your creativity, or anything else that you feel makes you an outstanding candidate.

Your Education: In this section, list the details of your college education (including the year of graduation and the degree you earned), your post-graduate education (if any), and other specialized education courses you've completed, such as a TEFL Certificate or teaching credential.

Your Work Experience: This information should be arranged chronologically, beginning with the most recent. Your work experience can include both paid and unpaid jobs, and you are also not obliged to, nor should you disclose every job you've ever had. You might want to discreetly omit the 3 weeks you spent delivering pizza and focus on the summer you spent volunteering for the Boys and Girls Club or tutoring math to high school students. Of course, if you've had more extensive teaching experience or related work experience, by all means be sure to highlight that in your resume.

Your Accomplishments: Look back over your life and compose a list of all the awards, certificates, and recognitions you've received in both your academic and professional career. It's okay to tap into ancient history here, as long as it's not too juvenile. Don't forget things like the National Honor Society, the Student of the Year awards, and the first place ribbons for your essays or poetry.

Your Personal Pursuits: Your hobbies say a lot about who you are, especially if they are academically or culturally related. Things like cooking international cuisine, leisure reading about Asian culture, a collection of antique kimonos, or a passion for Japanese *ukiyo-e* woodblock prints demonstrate your ongoing interest in culture and learning.

Your References: When deciding upon your references, be sure choose articulate, professional people who can attest to your integrity and work history. A college professor is more convincing than a next-door neighbor; and a former employer who likes you and respects your work is the most convincing reference of all. In addition to the name, address, phone, fax and e-mail address for each of your references, be sure to include their company names, their professions and titles, and the nature of your relationship with them.

A Picture is Worth ¥250,000 Yen: No matter where you choose to seek employment, competition is fierce, and anything you can do to make yourself stand out from the crowd increases your chances of getting hired. And although employers don't necessarily make their decisions based on looks, having a face to associate with a name helps to reinforce the connection between a personnel manager and a prospective employee. A photo on your resume serves the twofold purpose of making your face a familiar one to those in a position to hire you, and later reminds them of who you are once you've met them for an interview. So find the best picture you have of yourself, or have one taken specifically for this purpose, scan a high-resolution copy of it and paste it into the upper right or left hand corner of your resume. You'll be pleasantly surprised when you're the one they hire.

Japanese Glossary

The following is a list of the definitions of Japanese words that have been used throughout the text.

Arigato – Thank you

Arubaito – a part-time job, usually for students

Asoka – a conversational expression meaning, "Is that so?"

Dai Butsu – a large statue of Buddha

Domo arigato – Thank you very much.

Edo – the late 19th century era in Japan

Eigo no sensei – English teacher

Furo – a deep Japanese bathtub for soaking

Gaijin – foreigner

Ganbatte – Go for it! Give it your best effort.

Geta – wooden sandals

Gohan – cooked rice

Gomen nasai – Excuse me. Forgive me.

Hajime mashite – Nice to meet you.

Hanten – a short, open front cotton robe

Honto ni – a conversational expression meaning, "Really?"

Izakaya – a Japanese pub

Juku – an English cram school

Karaoke – recorded music without lyrics for the purpose of singing along.

Kaitenzushi – serve-yourself sushi on a conveyor

Kimono – a traditional formal robe

Kisaten – a coffee shop

Kotatsu – a low table with a heater attached to the underside for warming legs and feet

Kudasai – Please

Mansion – a modern apartment building

Mawashi – a loincloth

Mushi-atsui – steamy hot weather

Nihon do – the Japanese way

Obi – a wide sash

Ohanami – cherry blossom viewing

Ohayo – Good Morning.

Omikoshi – a portable Shinto shrine

Omiyage – souvenir gifts

Oshogatsu – the Japanese New Year's Holiday - December 25 - January 5

Otsukarisama deshita – We did it! Time to celebrate.

Oyayubi – the Japanese word for thumb, literally meaning "parent finger,"

Rabu hoteru – the Japanese phonetic translation of "love hotel"

Ramen – noodle soup

Ryokan – a traditional Japanese family-style inn.

Seiko o inorimasu – Good luck. I wish you success.

Sento – the public baths

Soroban – abacus

Tatami – finely woven rice straw floor mats, usually one meter wide by two meters long. Also a unit of measure for the area of a room.

Tsunami – tidal wave

Tomodachi – friend

Ukiyo-e – literally translated as "floating world," a term used to describe the idyllic life of the Edo period.

Usagi no uchi – rabbit warrens

Yakitori – grilled chicken on a stick

Yakuza – Japanese mobsters

Yukata – a cotton robe worn in summer

Wa – a spirit of harmony and cooperation

Address terminology

Ken – a prefecture

Ku – a ward within a prefecture

Chome – a neighborhood within a ward

Ban – a city block

Go – an individual building

Notes:

Resources, Bibliography, Webliography & Glossary

Afterword: Vignettes of Japan

My time in Japan left an indelible imprint on my life. The simple act of waking up each day was filled with possibility…countless opportunities to observe, to learn, and to be inspired. In Japan, one need only move through the day with a mindful eye, a willing spirit, and an open heart. Among the thousands of experiences I enjoyed during my stay, these are the ones I remember most fondly:

Gomen Nasai

Before I went to Japan, I was already familiar with the culture and had studied the two basic alphabets, however I only knew how to speak a few words of the language. My vocabulary consisted mostly of "*kudasai*," "*arigato*," and the names of my favorite kinds of sushi. But I had neglected to learn any of the practical phrases that would get me through an average day. And when preparing for the trip, I tried to pack light but still ended up with several large pieces of luggage; and I insisted on bringing my guitar, although I never played it that often. When we landed in Japan, my companion and I took the Keisei Skyliner from Narita Airport to Ueno Station in Tokyo, with our eventual destination being the home of a friend who lived way out in the suburb of Oji.

The trip required several train changes, and each time a train stopped for us to board or debark, we had to quickly transfer our two sets of luggage from the platform onto the train, or vice versa, in the few seconds before the doors closed again and the train took off. It was touch and go at every junction, but we had managed so far to successfully board the final train with all of our luggage in tow. Just one more stop and we'd be home free.

When the train finally pulled into Oji Station and the doors slid open, I was poised to make my move, and without looking, I heaved my oversized suitcases onto the platform. Little did I know that a diminutive Japanese businessman was waiting just a little too close to the door, and I bowled him right over with my luggage. Never before or since, have I been at such a loss for words. I was mortified. Of course I helped him up with many a chagrined apology in English, but what I wouldn't have given in that regretful moment to have known how to say, "*Gomen nasai!*"

Soroban

Japan is a paradox of ancient traditions and modern devices coexisting within a single society. It's not unusual to see an *Edo*-style temple standing next to a contemporary office building, or a crew of field workers, ankle deep in water, planting a rice paddy with high-rise buildings reflected in its mirrored surface. One day, while standing on the train platform waiting for the express train to Shinjuku Station, I witnessed the very best paradox of all.

The train platforms in Japan typically have a kiosk that sells sundries such as newspapers, cigarettes, umbrellas, souvenirs, candy, snacks, and beverages to busy commuters. Another convention in Japan is the use of the abacus, which the Japanese call *soroban*, as means of calculating figures. Postal clerks, shopkeepers, and even some bank tellers use them in the course of everyday transactions. School children learn the basics of the abacus, however, to use one professionally requires a skillful technique, almost like playing a musical instrument. Therefore, many Japanese people take special advanced classes to learn how to use an abacus properly.

What, you may ask, do a train platform kiosk and an abacus have to do with each other? Well on this particular day, while standing on the platform at Ikebukuro Station waiting for the express train to take me to my job in Shinjuku, I spotted an old woman, the proprietor of a sundries kiosk, bent over a computer-generated spreadsheet printed on that familiar green and white striped, accordion-folded paper with the perforated edges. I didn't think anything of it at first. She was just an old Japanese woman in an apron, perhaps doing her monthly bookkeeping. But upon closer observation, I realized that she was checking the rows and columns of figures on the computer spreadsheet…with an *abacus*!

Love Hotel

Kicking around the city of Tokyo and checking out various neighborhoods was my favorite way to spend Sunday afternoons. One sunny Sunday, I decided to explore my own neighborhood instead, and headed over to Higashi Ikebukuro, just across the tracks of the Yamanote Line from where I lived. I was on my way to the Sunshine 60 Building, which at that time was the tallest skyscraper in Asia, and along the way, I passed a Baskin & Robbins ice cream parlor. It was a warm day, and the temptation was just too great to resist, so I ordered myself a scoop of butter pecan and went back outside to enjoy it in the sunshine.

I'd also heard that this particular part of town was known for a stretch of love hotels, and I soon discovered that from the plaza where I sat eating my ice cream cone, I was looking right at it. Even if you've never been to one, the term "love hotel," or *rabu hoteru* as the Japanese call them, is self-explanatory. The rooms in these establishments rent by the hour and often feature fantasy-theme décor. Love hotels have names like *Dreamland* and *Yes Yes*, and the parking garages are discreetly hidden from view by drive through curtains. One can well imagine a love hotel as the site of many an infidelity, but in Japan, where single adults often still live with their parents, it's the perfect place to consummate young love.

People-watching has always been one of my favorite pastimes, and Tokyo is an excellent venue for it. On this particular day, I spotted an attractive young Japanese couple standing on the sidewalk outside one of the aforementioned love hotels. They seemed to be deliberating or negotiating over what I could only guess was whether or not to go in and get a room. This went on for several minutes, with the young man tugging gently at the young lady, doing his best to persuade her. The young lady, all the while, was coyly resisting. Finally, the young man won her over and they quickly ducked into the entrance. For the next few seconds, with my eyes still fixed on the spot where they'd stood, I sat smiling at the scene I'd just witnessed, when all of a sudden, out they came again. The young man shook his head, threw up his hands, and turned on his heel, with the young lady pleading sheepishly after him. After a few steps, he put his arm lovingly around her shoulder, she buried her face in his jacket, and off they went.

Omikoshi

Amid all its ultra-modern innovations, at its very heart, Japan is still a land of ancient tradition. Each region has its own unique cultural attributes, and most, if not all of their holidays and celebrations are based on some practice that dates back to the earliest days of its civilization. The Japanese celebrate the ephemeral cherry blossoms in spring, they celebrate the vernal and autumnal equinoxes, they celebrate the rice harvest, they celebrate the full moon, they celebrate the Emperor's birthday, and they celebrate the returning spirits of the deceased.

One day, while out and about in the suburb of Ikebukuro, I witnessed one of the liveliest and most dazzling celebrations of all: the Omikoshi parade. It was a beautiful afternoon, and I was headed over to the east side to buy a meter of cloth, when quite unexpectedly, I found myself in the midst of a throng of spectators lining the sidewalk. Over the tops of their heads, I could see an enormous and elaborately embellished structure bobbing along the parade route. It looked something like a miniature temple building, splendidly decorated with Japanese crests and golden filigree. I pushed my way through the crowd for a closer look and discovered that this colossal edifice was actually being heaved along the city streets on the shoulders of about a dozen strapping young Japanese men. What's more, they were dressed in traditional garb, which consisted of short, open-front robes called *hanten*, and white cotton loincloths called *mawashi*, which left their naked chests and buttocks quite exposed.

I was transfixed. I had never seen such an unabashed display of flesh and sinew. All those gorgeous young men, chanting in unison, laboring and sweating in the noonday sun, to transport the statue of their Shinto deity through the streets of Higashi Ikebukuro. It was...spectacular!

English a la Carte

To say that the Japanese are naïve in their use of English would be a kindly euphemism, when in fact, what I mean to say is that there were days when I wanted to go out and edit the entire city of Tokyo. In Japan, English in any form is trendy and hip, whether speaking it with foreigners, singing it in *karaoke* bars, or sporting it on some personal accessory. A word or two of it emblazoned on a handbag or a piece of clothing is *tres chic*. Which would be fine, except that its use in Japanese fashion, advertising, and product packaging is often either woefully out of context, or it's a bunch of incomprehensible gibberish.

Some days I was able to enjoy the humor of it, other days it drove me crazy. I couldn't help but chuckle to myself when I saw something like, "This is boy: Pretty wow guy!" printed on a teenager's knapsack. But there were times when it seemed that everywhere I looked, there was a shopping bag, a product label, a bus placard or a billboard that had shamelessly butchered my mothertongue.

One day the cosmos sent me a little gift that would allow me to transcend the issue once and for all, and never let it bother me again.

It was a workday, and I was on my way out of the building to take my lunch break. The school where I worked was located directly across from the east entrance of Shinjuku Station, above which there are several large department stores, including one called My City, which I could see from the entrance of the building. On this particular afternoon, parked in the loading zone of My City, was a small, white delivery truck, which I guessed must belong to some kind of clothing or accessory designer. The name of the company was printed in stylish lettering on the side of the truck, with the year in which it had been established proudly displayed beneath it.

It said: INFINITY...Since 1987.

Geisha with a Mohawk

On any given day, you never know who you're going to see when you're out and about in Tokyo. On a rainy weekday, it might be a group of Japanese kindergarten children on their way to an educational event, all wearing bright yellow rain slickers. On a Sunday afternoon in the off season, it might be a couple of gargantuan Sumo wrestlers dressed in their blue and white *yukata*, and wooden *geta*, heading back to the stable after a day in downtown Shinjuku. You might catch a glimpse of a Buddhist monk, head bowed under his straw lampshade of a hat, or a company baseball team in matching uniforms on their way to engage in the harmony of spirit known as *wa*.

The traditional Japanese lifestyle is a serene and conservative one, in which conformity and group mentality is key. At opposite ends of the contemporary spectrum, some individuals still live within the bounds of the strictest of classical tradition and dress accordingly, while many members of the younger generation strive to declare their independence with a bold fashion statement. Most of the population falls somewhere in between, dressing stylishly yet conservatively in western-style clothing. Still, the extremes are there to be observed on occasion.

One day, while riding the Yamanote, I was struck by the beauty of a Japanese woman in full *kimono*, one of deep blue floral silk, bound at the midriff by a bright orange *obi*. Her hair was meticulously coifed, her face was powdered to perfection with pure white rice dust, and her lips were painted with brilliant red precision. She was stunning and although I tried not to stare, I couldn't take my eyes off her. She was like a rare and exotic flower, and I could only wonder who she was and where she was going dressed like that.

The seat next to her was empty, and at the next station, a young man boarded the train and sat down beside her. In all my life, I have never seen such a contrast in humanity. The young man was dressed in what the Japanese call *panku stairu*, an expression literally borrowed from the English term "punk style." He was all black leather and chains from his knee-high boots to his skin-tight pants and open vest, and he wore the requisite studded bands around his neck and wrists. His costume was unoriginal, and certainly nothing that I hadn't seen dozens of times in San Francisco's Castro District, except that this young man's crowning glory was a bright orange Mohawk, varnished with hair gel until it stood straight up from his scalp to an altitude of at least a foot. He was magnificent.

So there they sat, the Geisha and the Punk, side by side on the Yamanote, neither taking any particular notice of each other, but creating a snapshot that will live forever in my mind's eye.

Mystery Men

The daily route from my apartment in Ikebukuro to the school where I taught in Shinjuku was quite unremarkable. The walk to the station every day was probably a little under a mile, most of it through small neighborhood streets lined with commonplace homes, ordinary shops and generic office buildings. But after a few months of walking the same path from home to the train station to the office and back again, I came to know every streetlamp and manhole cover. The faces of the neighborhood proprietors grew familiar and each day as I passed them, I would say *Ohayo* to Ohara-san, the lady whose family owned the convenience market, and to the butcher on the corner whose name I never learned, and to Ka-chan, the chef of a little neighborhood restaurant called *Ganbe*.

There was one place in particular, however, that remained a mystery. It was a building in the middle of the block, the entrance of which was always secured by a heavy gray roll-down door. In all the times I'd passed by, it was never open and there was never a soul to be seen. So imagine my surprise one Saturday evening when I rounded the corner to find that the mystery door had been lifted and there was a party going on inside. Not just an ordinary party, mind you, but a decidedly Japanese, male-only, sake-drinking party. The interior of the building was one big, empty *tatami* room that had been decorated for the occasion with floral wreaths, and colorful paper lanterns and streamers. About two dozen old men, dressed in traditional Japanese robes, were sitting around on cushions talking and singing and drinking; and although it was raining buckets outside, I couldn't help but stop to stare at them. As I stood there under my umbrella, feet soaking in puddles of rain, wondering what the cause for celebration was, one of the old men gestured for me to come inside and join them. I was overcome with curiosity, and it certainly looked like a lot more fun than trudging back home to an empty apartment, so I did.

I closed my umbrella, took off my shoes and sat down on the *tatami* floor. The old man who had invited me in grinned at me and filled my cup with hot sake. I soon discovered that nobody in the entire group spoke a word of English, so I fished my pocket dictionary out of my bag and made an attempt to communicate with them in Japanese. By this time, I'd been in Japan long enough to have mastered the basics of the language and could carry on simple conversations, although I never did become fluent enough to say anything intelligent or profound.

For the next couple of hours, I enjoyed the revelry and hospitality of those old men, and managed to convey to them that I was an English teacher from California. They all seemed rather impressed with that, and I became the subject of much head nodding and many an, "*Asoka.*" and a "*Honto ni?*" But try as I might, I never learned who those old men were and what they were celebrating. I still wonder to this day.

Tanabata

Japanese folklore is some of the world's most delightful literature, and during my stay in Japan, I read quite a bit of it, mostly about foxes and how they can change shapes and bewitch anyone who looks into their eyes. But my favorite Japanese folktale is the story of Tanabata, which has nothing to do with foxes. The Japanese version of the story is based on a romantic Chinese tale about a handsome young cowherd and a beautiful weaver.

As the story goes, each night the celestial maiden and her beautiful sisters weave the starry tapestry of the night sky; and each day the seven sisters come down to earth to bathe in a pond near the cowherd's pasture. One day, the cowherd spies the celestial maiden, and while she bathes, he steals the magical robe that gives her the power to fly. When the sisters finish bathing, they take to the skies again, and the celestial maiden is left behind. When the young cowherd comes to her rescue, the maiden is sad because she cannot return home, so she stays with the cowherd and soon falls in love with him.

Over time however, they realize that the sun no longer sets, and there is no nighttime for rest and sleep because the maiden is not there to help her sisters weave the tapestry of the night sky. It is then that the cowherd confesses the theft of her robe, and the maiden knows that she must bid her lover goodbye and return to her home in the sky.

But the maiden is so sad that, as she works her shuttle, her tears fall on the tapestry, each one creating a twinkling star. Over time, she cries so many tears that they become a river of stars. Meanwhile, back on earth the cowherd too is sad. However, a kindly magpie takes pity on him, and once a year, on the seventh day of the seventh month, the magpie enlists the aid of his flock to create a bridge of wings across the river of stars so that the two lovers can be together for one special night.

In the night sky, you can see the two lovers, Orihime the weaver, and Hikoboshi the cowherd, as two bright stars, Vega and Altair, separated by the starry river of the Milky Way. And every year, on the seventh of July, the Japanese celebrate Tanabata, which means Seven Evenings, by decorating the streets with pink streamers tied to the ends of long bamboo poles. The whole city turns pink with them, and lovers write special prayers on tiny pieces of paper and tie them to the streamers in hopes that they will be carried up to heaven where their wishes will be granted by the gods. It's a tale and a celebration of romance quite unlike any other.

Hanabi

When translated literally, *hanabi*, the Japanese word for fireworks, means *flower-fire*, and you haven't lived until you've seen fireworks in Japan. On warm evenings throughout the summer season, along the banks of Japan's rivers, the night sky explodes in bursts of fiery color. In fact, these fireworks displays are named for the riverbanks from which they are launched: *Tamagawa Hanabi, Kanagawa Hanabi, Sumidagawa Hanabi.*

By mid afternoon on the day of the fireworks, the rivers are already dotted with sailboats, motorboats and rowboats, all vying for the best location from which to view the spectacle. Rooftops are a popular spot for those lucky spectators with access to a place above the crowd. But mostly, the streets are jam-packed with common folk who have come to enjoy the festivities.

Along its length, as it winds its way through rural Japan and the suburbs of Tokyo, the Sumida River is crossed by many bridges, some of which are quite close together. The Sumidagawa Hanabi are launched over two such bridges, creating a doubly dazzling spectacle. On the day that I was fortunate enough to attend this fireworks display, my companion and I headed for the Sumida River after work and arrived with little time to spare. Having been offered no invitation to a private rooftop party, we were clueless as to where to view the display, and therefore had to rely on our intuition. We followed the general migration of the crowd toward what we guessed were the banks of the river. Block by block, as we drew nearer, the crowds became progressively thicker, moving more and more slowly, until we finally reached a standstill, packed like the proverbial sardines, unable to move in any direction.

Ordinarily, I would have worked myself into a state of panic over the closeness of the crowd, but at that moment, there was a deafening boom. The fireworks had begun. The world around me disappeared as I turned my gaze heavenward. It seems that, as we were propelled along by the crowds, we had somehow magically landed in the epicenter of the event. For the next 90 minutes, we were cascaded with shower after shower of brilliantly sparkling bursts of *flower-fire* on our upturned faces: an experience that defies description with mere words. But imagine, if you will, the biggest, grandest finale of a fireworks show you've ever seen. Multiply that by an hour and a half of non-stop pyrotechnics, and you might come close to picturing the explosive grandeur of the Sumidagawa Hanabi.

Somewhere Over the Rainbow

If someone had told me at age twenty-one, that twelve years later, I would have a baby in Japan, I'd have told them that they were quite crazy. But that's exactly what happened. It wasn't in the original plan, but then destiny never pays much heed to the small devices of us mortals. When I first suspected that I was pregnant, I lived in denial for weeks. During our winter vacation in Hawaii, I told myself that the fact that I didn't look so hot in a bikini anymore was just a symptom of spending my days with my bottom planted in chair all day, and a few too many Japanese sweet buns. But after the third month, I took a "sick day" from work and went to the American Clinic across from the Tokyo Tower. It was there that I finally admitted to myself what I already knew. I was pregnant.

On the way back home, I was so dazed by the notion that I got all the way to Senkawa Station on the Yurakucho Line before I realized that I had completely missed my stop at Ikebukuro. By now it was evening and time to face the music. When I arrived home, I took out a piece of red origami paper. On it I drew a big heart, and inside the heart I wrote the words, "When does 1+1=3?" I taped it to the front door and waited.

We decided to stay and have the baby in Japan, and in honor of the upcoming event, on the first day of May, while vacationing in Tochigi Prefecture, we got married at the ward office in the lovely alpine town of Nikko. Later that summer, we revisited the *Dai Butsu* at Kamakura, and this time, through a little hatch door at the back, I went down into the belly of the great statue. To be standing inside the belly of the Buddha with my baby stirring in my own belly was a truly blessed moment.

My pregnancy was idyllic, with no morning sickness or other discomfort, and I continued teaching until my eighth month. I grew quite rotund in those last weeks, especially when the baby didn't arrive on schedule. Fourteen anxious days later, on August 28th, I awoke in a puddle at six a.m. and realized that my water had broken. I was in labor. With my contractions coming about thirty minutes apart, we calmly got dressed and walked down to the corner to hail a taxi to take us to Seibo Byoin, a nearby Catholic hospital.

We spent the afternoon in a comfortable private room, with my contractions growing steadily closer and closer together until I thought that it would drive me mad. It's not that I was in any great pain per se, it's just that there was never enough time to rest in between. The hospital provided me with my own private midwife, who coached me through every breath. She recommended that I choose an object and focus on it while I breathed through each contraction. There was a small window above my hospital bed, and at about five p.m., after I'd focused on every object in the room, and breathed through what seemed like a thousand contractions, I turned toward that window and fixed my gaze on the Tokyo skyline. And that's when I saw it: The biggest, brightest, most glorious rainbow I'd ever seen, arching radiantly over the city.

At 6:22 p.m., the moment finally came when I held my baby boy in my arms and looked into his eyes for the first time. I can say without hesitation that it was the greatest moment of my life. He was perfect in every way: healthy, beautiful, and pure as a dewdrop. We named him Will. Not for William, but for a concept conceived by Kurt Vonnegut in his novel *The Sirens of Titan*, known as *The Universal Will To Become*.

Oyayubi

Japan is a culture with many superstitions, especially surrounding death and the funereal ceremony that follows. Japanese funerals are highly stylized rites, conducted by Buddhist priests according to the traditions of the Buddhist religion. A wake is held for the deceased, during which friends and family come to pay their respects. A special meal is served, and afterwards, the immediate family and close friends accompany the body of the deceased to the crematorium.

Many symbolic rituals are performed during the mourning process. For purification, a small mound of salt is placed on the threshold of the home of the deceased. In some cases, after cremation, family members use chopsticks to pass the charred remains of the deceased from person to person, until they are placed at last in the crematory urn for burial. An offering of food is often placed on the graves of the deceased, with a pair of chopsticks standing upright in it.

One of the strangest superstitions associated with the funeral ceremony is the practice of hiding one's thumbs by wrapping the other fingers around them whenever a funeral procession passes by.

The Japanese word for thumb is *oyayubi*, which, when literally translated, means "parent finger." According to Japanese superstition, if you happen to see a funeral procession passing by and you forget to hide your thumbs, you will not be present to comfort your parents when they die.

My father died while I was in Japan. I knew that he was ill, and for that reason I paid a farewell visit to my hometown to see him one more time before I left for Tokyo. I'll never forget him standing in the doorway of my childhood home, waving goodbye. I didn't know it then, but that would be the last time I ever saw him.

About three months after my son was born, I was beginning to feel like myself again, and the prospect of making the trip home to see my parents didn't seem so impossible anymore. One evening, I decided that I was ready to bring my baby home to meet them, so I hopped on my bicycle and headed over to the Hotel Metropolitan to use the international pay telephone. When I called my parents' house to tell them the good news, my older sister answered the phone, and I immediately asked how my father was doing. After a .short but dreadful pause, she said, "Oh no, you don't know..." She gave the phone to my mother, who tearfully told me that my father had died ten days earlier, and had already been buried. In that instant, all joy was extinguished.

It seems that our nameplate had fallen off the mailbox, and when the Western Union deliveryman came with the telegram, he couldn't figure out which apartment was ours, so he left without delivering it. I didn't learn of my father's death until that fateful evening almost two weeks later. Such a cruel twist of fate. Much of my memory after that is a blur, but somehow I remember thinking on the long ride home, that I must have forgotten to hide my thumbs.

Sayonara

Every foreigner who has ever lived in Japan realizes at some point that it's time to go. We all have our reasons. After the death of my father, I fell into a deep depression, and one day, while vacantly watching particles of dust dance on a beam of sunlight over a cup of tea in the *tatami* room, I knew that going home was my only salvation. So I bought myself a one-way ticket to San Francisco, packed up my baby and my belongings and bade farewell to the life that I had so loved in Tokyo. It was one of the most difficult decisions I have ever made.

After a short stopover in California, I spent the next three months at my parents' house in my hometown of Mobile, Alabama with my son Will. One summer afternoon, I visited the cemetery and planted a dogwood tree on my father's grave.

Over time, I found joy again. Upon my return to the Napa Valley, I became a private tutor to the children of Japan Airlines flight instructors living with their families in the U.S. My son has grown into a brilliant young man, and has even returned to Japan for a visit to his birthplace. I still miss my father every day, and I miss Japan just as often. But life is good, and Japan will still be there in all its grace and splendor when I am ready to return.